CW00708016

Translated by
Will Sleath

© 2007 by goldfinch books, Hamburg/Germany

All rights reserved.
No part of this publication may be reproduced, stored in a retrieval system or transmitted in any form by any means, electronic, mechanical, photocopying, recording or otherwise, without the prior permission in writing by the publisher, except brief extracts for the purpose of review.

Editor: Julia Kaufhold
Text, research & photos: Julia Kaufhold
Translation: Will Sleath, St Ives
Illustrations & maps: Nicola Clark, St Ives
Layout & typesetting: TypoWerkstatt Timon Schlichenmaier, Hamburg
Printing & binding: Kösel GmbH & Co. KG, Altusried-Krugzell/Germany

All information in this book has been collected by the author, is correct to the best of her knowledge and has been carefully checked by the publisher, but incorrect content cannot be totally excluded. The publisher thus emphasises that all information is without guarantee in terms of product liability, and that no responsibility or liability can be assumed for any inconsistencies. Comments about quality are the purely subjective opinion of the author and are not intended as publicity for companies and products. We request your understanding in this matter, and will always be grateful for any ideas and suggestions.

www.goldfinchbooks.de

1st edition April 2007

ISBN 978-3-940258-01-4

St Ives
and trips in the vicinity

Julia Kaufhold

with illustrations by Nicola Clark

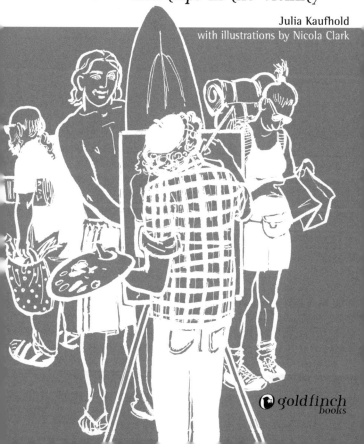

goldfinch
books

CONTENTS

Interviews

SEEKING THE SECRET OF ST IVES

Written descriptions of St Ives all sound very similar, praising its picturesque harbour, narrow cobbled alleys, fantastic beaches and, not least,
its art. Here, too, one can only *attempt* to explain the town's magical
attraction, because **St Ives is unique and words cannot describe it** – at
least not directly.

A crucial feature is the geographical situation of St Ives and the ines-
capable awareness of being at the very end of the country. After the
Penwith peninsula, apart from the Isles of Scilly **there is nothing but
sea all the way to America**. But because you can never see beyond the
horizon everything which may or may not lie behind it is left to the in-
finite scope of the imagination.

The light in St Ives, which has been described as 'extremely clear' and
'highly conducive to painting', is above all changeable. The peripheral
location of the town means that the weather and thus the colour of

the sky and the sea change by the minute. Stunning cloud formations break in the sea, which is by turns rough and calm, and alternate between perfect turquoise und ominous grey. **Seldom are the forces of nature so tangible.**

The feeling of breadth and the enormous drama of the place release boundless creative energy. It feels as if you are absorbing the surroundings. Small wonder, then, that St Ives became a **top artists' colony**; indeed, in the 50s New York and St Ives were the most important artists' colonies in the world. **And to this day West Cornwall is home to more artists than anywhere else in the UK outside London.** The creative conflicts concentrated on this very small area, which used to give rise to new developments, are now fewer in number, but here and there you can still encounter excellent artists and works. And even watercolour views of the harbour have their place, representing a delightful and idyllic opposing pole to tension and drama.

The geographical location is also responsible for the mild climate and the picturesque nature of the area. The influence of the Gulf Stream gives Cornwall an early spring and a long summer, and creates a practically **frost free microclimate in which subtropical plants can flourish**.

But evidently the town was not always as beautiful as it is today. **St Ives was even said to stink and to sadden people:**

> 'St Ives does not benefit from closer inspection. Despite its beautiful situation, its narrow, winding alleys seem inclined to sadden visitors and drive away illusions. It is a fishing village through and through. Nearly all the houses have stone steps outside leading to the first floor, where the families live, whilst the ground floor is occupied by fish cellars. The latter give off odours which penetrate the inhabited part of the house – odours that are anything but pleasant, especially during the pilchard season.'
> From: Alphonse Esquiros *Cornwall and its Coasts*, 1865.

For centuries St Ives lived from its pilchard catch – in 1905 13 million fish were caught in a single day using only five nets. At that time the town was indeed very loud, crowded and full of fish (and fishy smells), but at the beginning of the 20th century the pilchards suddenly found another route for their early-summer migration, and the great fishing era came to an abrupt close. St Ives – named after the Irish missionary St Ia, who is said to have sailed over from Ireland on a leaf in the 5th century – was at the time already an artists' colony and centre of tourism, as if by way of compensation.

St Ives now caters for all tastes: Walkers have the coastal path on their doorstep and **surfers** the big waves, and there are palms for **fans of the Mediterranean** and four beaches (five including Carbis Bay) for **sun worshippers** and **sand castle builders**. There are shipwrecks for **divers** to explore and fine dining for **gourmets**. **Art lovers** only need to peep round the next corner to find another gallery – Tate St Ives being the crowning glory. A wander through the former fishing quarter *Downalong* and a visit to an old tin mine are enriching experiences not only for out-and-out **history enthusiasts**, just as the annual September Festival does not only attract **musicians**. **Rosamunde Pilcher fans** can indulge in cream teas and **authors** ruminate over a Cornish pasty. And even before everywhere has closed down for the day everyone comes swarming back into town, gagging for a nice pint in one of the many pubs.

A haven for relaxed people
Mo Scott is someone who returns every season to work in St Ives.

Why? St Ives is a haven for relaxed people. Everything is close at hand and everyone knows everyone. You meet so many people here from all over the world, and age is totally irrelevant. It's just nice!
Spot: Man's Head.
Beach: Porthmeor Beach.
Activity: Walk to Zennor.
Restaurant: St Andrews Street Bistro.
Pub: Golden Lion.
Evening pursuit: Camp fire on Porthmeor Beach.

1 Bus Station
2 Railway Station
3–5 Post Office
6–10 Bank
11 Tourist Information Centre (TIC)
12 Cinema
13 Library
14–17 Supermarket
18 Tate Gallery
19 Barbara Hepworth Museum
20 Leach Pottery
21 Arts Club
22 Hospital
23 Police Station

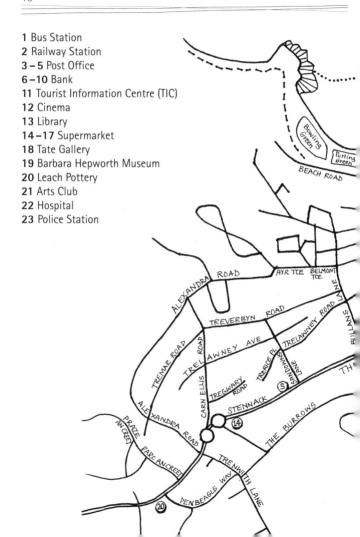

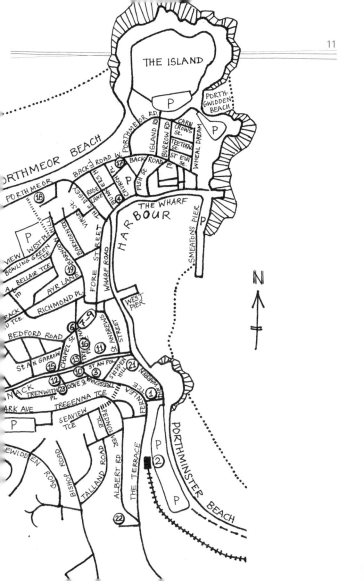

Getting there

BY CAR

Turn off the M5 onto the A30 towards Exeter at Exit 31 (Exeter South). Then simply continue on the A30 to Hayle. Just after Hayle take the second roundabout exit onto the A3074, signposted to St Ives. Go over the first mini roundabout, then turn right at the next one. Continue on the A3074 through Lelant, then on the St Ives Road through Carbis Bay. This road goes straight to St Ives.

Alternative: At the second mini-roundabout do not turn right into Lelant, but instead left onto the B3311 towards St Ives. After about 3 miles turn right at the big T-Junction and go through Halsetown. At the next T-Junction right again. This brings you into the town from the other side, on the B3306 coast road.

The A30 from Exeter to St Ives is usually the slowest part of the journey. **Traffic jams** at Indian Queens can easily hold you up by up to 2 hrs, especially at the weekend, but in the high season also during the week.

- **Outward-journey tip:** If at all possible get past this spot by 9am or after 7pm.
- **Return-journey tip:** To be on the safe side, leave St Ives by 7am or after 1pm. Most people leave for home between 8am and 11am, and the traffic gets pretty heavy then.

BY TRAIN

Train travel to St Ives is highly recommendable. The last section, from St Erth to St Ives, offers **unbelievable, heart-stopping views** over St Ives Bay. Sit on the right!

- **Information:** on Tel. 08457-484950 or www.national rail.co.uk. Book your tickets as early as possible, as they are far cheaper then.

BY COACH

Usually it takes longer than by train, but can be cheaper. Prices and travel times on Tel. 08705-808080 or at www.nationalexpress.co.uk.

Journey times to St Ives

Departure from	By train	By coach
London	5.5 hrs	8.5 hrs
Cardiff	6 hrs	8 hrs
Birmingham	6 hrs	8.5 hrs
Liverpool	8.5 hrs	12.5 hrs
Newcastle	9.5 hrs	15 hrs

(The above journey times are approximate.)

BY AIR
Newquay Airport is 40 miles from St Ives and is served by the following airlines:

Air Southwest Flies from Gatwick, Manchester, Leeds Bradford (all three from £38 single), Bristol, Cardiff (from £27) and Dublin (from £30) – all prices including taxes and charges, www.airsouthwest.com.

Ryanair From Stansted (from about £24 each way including taxes and charges), www.ryanair.de. Book early!

Bearing in mind the short distance, travel by public transport from Newquay to St Ives is not exactly an edifying experience.

Four ways of getting out of Newquay:
- **Coach:** Best option. By taxi or the No. 910 bus *(Summercourt Travel)* to Newquay Manor Road stop. Onward journey by coach, journey time 1¼ hrs, no changes but

fairly infrequent, from about £5, www.nationalexpress.com.

- **Bus:** A little sightseeing tour of the villages. From the Manor Road stop take the No. 89 or No. 90 bus to Truro (about 50 min.), then spend another 1½ hrs on the No. 14 to St Ives, www.firstgroup.com.
- **Train:** Journey time about 2½ hrs, two changes, from about £7.
- **Hire car:** Europcar (01872-266300) or Hertz (01637-860869) are right by Newquay Airport. Journey to St Ives about 45 min.

Accommodation

If you wish to gain an overview of the huge range of accommodation in St Ives and Carbis Bay the following two websites are particularly helpful:

- **www.stives-cornwall.co.uk:** Official website for St Ives in collaboration with the *St Ives Hotel & Guest House Association*. Accommodation divided into price categories and indicated on the town map.

- **www.visit-stives.co.uk:** Constantly updated information on beds available in the various types of accommodation.

Despite the wealth of accommodation offered, most of it gets taken early on, and above all in July and August St Ives is hopelessly overbooked. Following their summer stay, many visitors immediately reserve their B&Bs or holiday flats and cottages for the following year. So if you want to be assured of a bed you must book for the summer months as early as possible – preferably around Easter time. There's usually a better chance of getting something in Carbis Bay, though.

The **Tourist Information Centre** is extremely helpful when you're looking for somewhere to stay (see 'A-Z of Tips for Visitors').

Prices below marked 'from' apply to the low season. All prices include breakfast unless stipulated otherwise.

HOTELS
Leaves nothing to be desired
Blue Hayes Private Hotel
An oasis of relaxation, exclusivity and pampering. **What?** Fresh lilies, palm trees in the gardens, creamy-white furnishings and a breathtaking sea view to be enjoyed during breakfast or light supper on the terrace, with its panoramic view and Capri like feeling. Each of the five rooms has different special features (sea view, balcony, huge bath, four-poster bed etc.), and you choose the room when booking, referring to the views from every angle on the website.

Out-and-out luxury, but not overdone. **Why?**

How much?	From £70 pppn in double room, with first-class breakfast. Parking included.
Where?	Trelyon Avenue (5 min. to Porthminster Beach via the Southwest Coastal Path, 10 min. to the harbour), Tel. 01736-797129, www.bluehayes.co.uk.

All's well if you eat well

The Garrack Hotel & Restaurant

What?	Absolute comfort in a traditional country house. Beautiful gardens, a view of Porthmeor Beach to die for and the perfect starting point for cliff-top walks.
Why?	If only for the excellent food.
How much?	From £60 pppn in double room; from £72 pppn in single room. Full board also available, from £82 (4 course menu).
Where?	Burthallan Lane (about 15 min. by foot to the harbour/beach), Tel. 01736-796199, www.garrack.com.
Tip	The prize-winning restaurant with its fantastic sea view is also open to non-residents. Be sure to try the cheeseboard with its numerous Cornish, British and French cheeses. Chutney and plum bread are included, and the portions are huge!

Feel at home in Carbis Bay

Boskerris Hotel

What?	15 rooms with tasteful contemporary furnishings and en suite designer bathrooms. For guests who wish to be close to St Ives but far enough away from the madding crowd – an ideal and elegant oasis of calm. Overwhelming view of the whole of St Ives Bay, and not just from the Mediterranean style terrace. Buffet supper.

Because you immediately feel at home, thanks to the friendly and excellent, though never obtrusive service.

Why?

From £42.50 pppn in standard double room; from £62.50 pppn in superior double room.

How much?

Boskerris Road, Carbis Bay (5 min. to the beach, 1½ miles from St Ives on the coastal path), Tel. 01736-795295, www.boskerrishotel.co.uk.

Where?

Rich in history
Edgar's Private Hotel/Chy-an-Creet

Cosy little hotel with garden and plenty of room for relaxation. Inviting lounge with shelves full of books; a bar, with a nice fire blazing in the hearth when it's cold outside. All rooms have their own bath and TV.

What?

Put your feet up in this historic environment. The eponymous Edgar Skinner was the manager of the famous potter Bernard Leach. He built Chy-an-Creet as his private abode in about 1923.

Why?

From £31 pppn in double room; in single room from £45. Parking included (parking in St Ives is an extremely tricky matter).

How much?

Higher Stennack (straight opposite the Leach Pottery), Tel. 01736-796559, www.chy.co.uk.

Where?

BED & BREAKFAST/GUEST HOUSES

There are B&Bs and guest houses galore in the St
Ives Bay area. Many of them are in *Downalong* – the
former fishermen's quarter with its maze of picturesque cobbled streets and alleys right in the heart of
the town. In the immediate vicinity of the harbour,
beaches and main shopping street. NB: Not for claus-
trophobics, as many of these old cottages have the
typical low ceilings.

White Waves: Very pleasant Edwardian style B&B
with antique furniture, fabulous view of the harbour
and fresh fruit salad for breakfast. From £26 pppn in
double room. 4 Sea View Terrace, Tel. 01736-797374,
www.bedandbreakfaststives.com.

Downalong

someone
lives in here too!

Treliska: Very central – but quiet – B&B. Modern furnishings, very clean rooms with attention to detail. Excellent coffee. Around £30 pppn in double room. 3 Bedford Road, Tel. 01736-797678, www.connexions. co.uk/treliska.

Kynance: Former tin miner's cottage in perfect location with great sea view and beautiful terrace. All six rooms en suite. From £30 pppn in double room. The Warren, Tel. 01736-796636, www.kynance.com.

CHEAPER ALTERNATIVES
Relaxing
Zennor Backpackers

Lovely little 32 bed hostel in a former chapel, 10 min. from St Ives. Own café, where evening meals are also served. Ideal spot for walkers and those seeking relaxation.

What?

Because it's nicer, cleaner and less chaotic than the St Ives backpackers hostel, and because Zennor is a mystical, ancient granite village very close to the cliffs.

Why?

From £12 pppn in dormitories, breakfast £3-4.50 extra. No self-catering facilities.

How much?

The Old Chapel, Zennor (good bus connection to St Ives), Tel. 01736-798307, www.backpackers.co.uk/zennor.

Where?

(Youth) hostels in Cornwall

200 hostels in England and Wales belong to the *Youth Hostel Association (YHA)*, and ten of them are in Cornwall. They offer a surprisingly high standard and are in particularly beautiful buildings. Guests of all ages welcome. Unfortunately St Ives has no YHA hostel – a real shortcoming. Whet your appetite on the website: www.yha.org.uk

Nearby YHA hostels:

- **The Lizard:** Luxurious hostel at the southernmost extremity of the British mainland, and the starting point for one of England's most beautiful cliff walks: the walk to Kynance Cove, where you feel as if you're in the South Seas. From £15.50 pppn.
- **Perranporth:** Less luxurious but very atmospheric, in a former coastwatch station overlooking a huge sandy beach. From £13.95 pppn.

Private Hostels:

No uniform standard – can be very good (e.g. Zennor or Penzance), but are sometimes less enthralling. Comprehensive but impartial information on backpacking at www.backpaxmag.com and www.backpackers.co.uk.

Whether the hostel is private or YHA, advance booking is strongly recommended.

Camping with sea view
Ayr Holiday Park

The only camp site in St Ives. Very clean (including sanitary facilities). Spaces for tents, motorhomes and touring caravans, and high-quality holiday caravans for hire. Immediate access to coastal path, ideal location for cliff walks.

What?

Because you have a wonderful view of Porthmeor Beach from nearly everywhere in the site.

Why?

From £9.50 for 2 people with tent, from £13.50 with car and caravan.

How much?

Higher Ayr (10 min. by foot to the harbour), Tel. 01736-795855, www.ayrholidaypark.co.uk.

Where?

Poldhu B&B: Not exactly beautiful, but cheap. You can't get any more central. £18 pppn, including in single rooms and during the summer. 60 Fore Street, Tel. 01736-794226.

SELF-CATERING

To the hoteliers' chagrin, self-catering accommodation is gaining in popularity. For longer stays (especially for cooking fanatics) these holiday homes are thoroughly recommendable, as you don't have to eat out in a restaurant, so it's easier on your wallet. Rentals are nearly always by the week – usually Saturday to Saturday. For July/August it's a good idea to book the previous autumn. One week in the high season (August) costs from about £370 in the bottom price bracket (small one-bedroom cottage/flat).

There are many providers – both big and small – of holiday cottages and studios in St Ives.

Cornish Riviera Holidays: 70 cottages and holiday flats in the heart of St Ives through a friendly company. Westcott's Quay (opposite the Arts Club), Tel. 01736-797891, www.cornishrivieraholidays.co.uk.

St Ives Holidays/Lanhams: Biggest selection, with over 230 properties in all price ranges in St Ives, Carbis Bay and Lelant. High Street, Tel. 01736-794686, www.stives holidays.com.

Powells Cottage Holidays: Around 70 properties in St Ives, Carbis Bay and Lelant; 3- to 4-day stays also possible. Tel. 01834-812791, UK freephone 0800-378771, www.powells.co.uk.

Aspects Holidays: Around 170 properties in St Ives and Carbis Bay. The Wharf, Tel. 01736-794495, www. aspects-holidays.co.uk.

Food

Gourmet's delight
The restaurants of St Ives place great value on **top quality** and exclusive use of the freshest ingredients (frozen fish is simply not served), seasonal products and if possible regional produce.

As a visitor to this little coastal town you must be willing to experiment. The restaurants outbid each other with their **adventurous combinations**, and what does not at first seem appropriate is made appropriate.

And precisely because unusual combinations have become the general philosophy, the numerous eating places in St Ives are **actually quite uniform in their diversity** and do not differ that much from each other. The Italian restaurant offers a Bengali pizza with an Indian chicken tikka and mango sauce, the Chinese serves chips instead of rice with the chop suey and the traditional pub offers food with a Mediterranean twist.

On the menus all of this is reflected in a sometimes silly **linguistic confusion**. Grilled Cornish oysters are dished up with a wasabi (Japanese horseradish) mayonnaise and chorizo (Spanish paprika sausage), then there are vegetable fajitas (Mexican wheat tortillas) fried in a Chinese wok, served in an American frying pan and accompanied by salsa, guacamole and sour cream. Help!

And nevertheless, or maybe for this very reason, eating out in St Ives is a **gourmet's delight**. But after culinary cornucopia even the most ardent of foodies like getting back to basics and enjoying some good old bread and cheese.

Eating out in St Ives is expensive – there's just no denying it.
Skinflint thus recommends:

- Lower prices at or before certain times, so look out for **early-bird menus** and teatime or lunchtime specials (often advertised outside).
- Go out for **lunch instead of an evening meal** – the same dishes often much cheaper.
- **BYO**: In some restaurants in St Ives, even though they're fully licensed, you can still bring your own bottle and pay the £1 to £2 corkage. Enquire at the restaurant beforehand!
- Cheap and cheerful: Most pubs offer very good **bar meals**, which above all come in generous portions.

RESTAURANTS
Interesting concept
The Seafood Café

What?   Guests create their own menu here. Procedure: Select 1) Fish or meat, 2) Type of preparation, 3) Sauce (incl. strawberry & lime, peppers & mango, port & plum), 4) Type of potato (e.g. rocket & parmesan mash or early potatoes roasted in garlic and herbs).

Why?   Because the concept is good and the fish couldn't be fresher.

Lunch (set dishes) 12–3pm, evening meal from 6pm. **When?**
Do make a reservation!

Evenings: Fish and meat £9 to £17 including potatoes **How much?**
and sauce (vegetables extra).

45 Fore Street, Tel. 01736-794004, www.seafood **Where?**
cafe.co.uk.

A favourite haunt
Porthgwidden Café

More than a favourite restaurant or café – it is one of
the most beautiful places in St Ives. That's why many
locals come here to read a book over a cup of coffee.

Breakfast (e.g. scrambled eggs with smoked salm- **What?**
on for £5), wonderful snacks (highly recommended:
cranberry & brie baguette with home-made chips and

salad – likewise £5, and guaranteed to fill you up) and in the evening fish, meat, pasta of the day and vegetarian dishes.

Why? An oasis of wellbeing. The brilliant white of the terrace, the deep blue of the sea and the view of the rocky coastline give it a Greek feel. Inside, wooden floors and a relaxed, informal atmosphere.

When? From Easter (provided the artists who've rented the restaurant as a winter studio have vacated the premises) until about mid-October. Breakfast is served until 11am, lunch 12pm–3pm and evening meals 6pm–10pm. It's advisable to make evening bookings two to three days in advance (especially the window table!).

How much? £9–£13 for an evening main course.

Where? The only restaurant overlooking the small Porthgwidden Beach, Tel. 01736-796791, www.porthgwidden cafe.co.uk.

For Bohemians

St Andrews Street Bistro

What? Wonderful food! Successful because of its restrained marrying of *Modern British Food* with influences from the Middle East. The select curries (including vegetarian) are particularly delicious. Rick Stein thinks the St Andrews Street Bistro is one of the five best restaurants in the whole of Cornwall.

Why? Food and atmosphere in perfect symbiosis. Fine dining amidst unusual pictures by local artists, a collection of antique furniture, high ceilings with brightly coloured stucco – all bathed in the muted light of red lampshades.

When? In summer 7 days 11am–2pm and 6.30–10pm; in winter Wed–Sun 12–2pm and 7–9.30pm.

Main dishes £10 to £17 – good portions.   How much?
16 St Andrews Street (two minutes from the harbour),   Where?
Tel. 01736-797074.

At the home of the Austrian poet Evelyn Holloway the kitchen often remains cold.
Ever since 1995 she has commuted between St Ives and Vienna, alternating two months in each domicile, and she usually eats out.

The following are her personal tips:

Leisurely breakfast: Deli Café (Chapel Street).

Coffee and a book: Porthgwidden Café (Porthgwidden Beach).

Tasty delicacies: Presto (Fore Street), and very good coffee.

Urban atmosphere: If you wish to submit to the illusion of being in a big town just go to the Bistro (High Street) and watch the passers-by out shopping.

View: Pedn-Olva Hotel/Restaurant (The Warren).

Fish: Ocean Grill (Wharf Road).

Indian food: Rajpoot Restaurant (Gabriel Street).

Special treat: Saltwater Café (Fish Street). I always go there once when I'm over here.

Cheap & cheerful: Porthmeor Beach Café. You go there because of the beach.

Friendly service: St Andrews Street Bistro (St Andrews Street).

Evelyn has brought out two CDs: *Sky Walking* together with the gallery owner Bob Devereux, and *Letters from the Wilderness* with the musician Bernie Davies – both a combination of poetry and jazz. Available in the *Salthouse Gallery* (Norway Square).

Best breakfast
Ocean Grill

The full English breakfast is usually a rather greasy affair, but that's not the case at Ocean Grill. Choice ingredients are lavishly prepared here, and you can enjoy the wonderful view of the picturesque harbour whilst eating your food.

What? Two versions of the full English breakfast are offered. With meat: Thick slices of bacon with no fat, quality sausages, grilled mushrooms and tomatoes, baked beans, a choice of eggs and toasted ciabatta.
Without meat: Grilled tomatoes and mushrooms, fresh spinach and grilled early potatoes, a choice of eggs and toasted ciabatta. Also other breakfasts such as blueberry pancakes or scrambled eggs with salmon.

Why? Because there's no greasy residue on the plate.

When? 9–11am. Lunch 12pm–2.30pm, evening meal from 5.30pm, in winter from 6.30pm.

How much? Full English breakfast £6.25, vegetarian option £5.75.

Where? Wharf Road, first floor, Tel. 01736-799874, www.ocean-grill.co.uk.

TAKEAWAYS
Brilliant salad bar
Good Health takeaway

What? One of the very best things about St Ives. It offers freshly made salads and various kinds of bread, and you can compose your own filings from a huge range of fine ingredients. Plus excellent dressings (e.g. lime & coconut).

Because healthy food can be so tasty and vice versa. Top tip: Combine the small salad – which is actually not at all small – with hummus.	Why?
Mon-Sat from 10.30am–3.30pm (but sometimes later and sometimes earlier).	When?
A small salad costs £2.30, with hummus £2.60.	How much?
Tregenna Place.	Where?

In discussion with **Simon Pellow**, Head Chef and owner of **The Wave Restaurant**

What was your reason for opening a restaurant? I wanted to be able to do things my own way and so my wife and I would see each other.

What is your favourite food? At home: homemade Cornish Pasty, in a restaurant: squid.

What are your favourite ingredients to cook with? Fresh fish and good quality produce.

Cooking advices:
1. Use fresh produce.
2. Season well.
3. Simple dishes and flavours are often the best.

The Wave Restaurant
17 St Andrews Street
Tel. 01736-796661
www.wave-restaurant.co.uk

THE CORNISH PASTY

*'Page: Wife, bid these getlemen welcome. Come, we have **a hot ven-
ison pasty** to dinner: come gentlemen, I hope we shall drink down
all unkindness.'*
From: William Shakespeare *The Merry Wives of Windsor*, 1597.

In St Ives you just can't get away from Cornish pasties. These filled,
crescent shaped pastry pockets are available all over the place here,
and can involve every conceivable combination.

The pasty derives its typical shape from its origin as the **daily meal
of Cornish tin miners**. As tin mining often involved handling of the
poisonous substance arsenic and miners were unable to wash their
hands before every meal, to avoid poisoning they used to hold their
pasties by the crusty pastry edge, eat the filling and throw the rest
away. Hence Cornish pasties' thick crimping, which remains a feature.

Basic recipe for Cornish pasties
(four pasties)

Dough:
450 g strong plain flour
½ a teaspoon salt
100 g cold butter
100 g lard
(or 200 g butter)
approx. 175 ml cold water

First mix the flour with the salt in a large bowl. Then bit by bit work the chilled butter and the lard in well with your fingers. Whilst constantly stirring, add as little water as is necessary to create a workable and non sticky dough. Knead thoroughly with cold fingers, shape into a ball and place in the fridge for 45 minutes.

Filling:
300 g chuck steak or skirt
600 g potatoes
1–2 swedes
1 big onion
Salt, pepper, sugar

Cut the raw steak, the potatoes and the swedes into very small pieces, chop the onion finely and mix all the ingredients well. Add up to four table spoons of water or stock if necessary. Spice well with salt, pepper and a generous pinch of sugar.

Remove dough from fridge, divide into four portions and roll out into rounds on a floured surface. The rounds should have a diameter of 20–23cm.

Lay some of the prepared meat/vegetable mixture on one half of each of the rounds. Gently moisten the edges with cold water, fold the rounds of dough over and press together firmly. Coat with beaten egg and make holes in each pasty using a fork.

Bake at 220 °C in a preheated oven for about 20 minutes. Then reduce the temperature to 150 °C and bake for a further 20 minutes. Before serving let the pasties rest for ten minutes in the switched-off oven.

Superlative pasties
Pengenna Pasties

What?	The best, the biggest, the least fatty and the most freshly prepared pasties in St Ives. Choice of four classic types.
Why?	Because you have to close your eyes and hold your nose if you want to get past the shop without partaking.
When?	Daily 9am–5pm.
How much?	Vegetarian pasty for £2.50, with lamb £2.75.
Where?	9 High Street, www.pengennapasties.co.uk. Or place an order for delivery to your home address, Tel. 01288-355169 (minimum 12 pasties).

Variety guaranteed
Cornish Bakehouse

What?	Twelve different pasties – most of them are out of the ordinary: e.g. spicy chicken with marinated limes, mango chutney, raisins and yoghurt. Also sandwiches, baguettes and panini. Highly recommended: spicy vegetable whole-grain pasty with ginger and soy sauce, or broccoli & cheese pasty.
Why?	Because of the joy of culinary experimentation.
When?	Summer: Daily 9am–9pm (The Wharf until 11pm), Winter: Daily 9am–5pm (Wharf Road closed).
How much?	Broccoli & cheese pasty for £1.75, and small traditional beef pasty as a taster for 95p.
Where?	Three locations: 51 Fore Street and two shops on the harbour, The Wharf und Wharf Road, www.cornish bakehouse.com.

Watch out for those gulls!

Kingfisher

Not really a takeaway, but more an excellent fish'n'chip shop in a fast-food restaurant. | **What?**

The romantic idea of feasting on fish & chips on a bench by the harbour is rapidly destroyed by the greedy seagulls (particularly aggressive in the spring). So it's better to watch the battle for food from a safe haven and enjoy your meal in peace. | **Why?**

During the season 12-9pm, otherwise 12–6.30pm. | **When?**

Fish & chips £4.90, small portions (not only for children and actually not small) for £3.90. | **How much?**

Wharf Road, on the first floor. | **Where?**

DON'T FEED THE SEAGULLS!

CORNISH CREAM TEA

An absolute must for anyone visiting St Ives is a Cornish cream tea, comprising scones, clotted cream and jam. Argument is rife both about the origin of the cream tea (Cornwall or Devon) and the pronunciation of the word scone (short or long vowel), but as far as the origin is concerned we'll plump for Cornwall.

Make it yourself:
Clotted cream is normally made from unhomogenised cow's milk, but as this is not always available here is a replacement **recipe:**
Mix two parts of whole milk with one part of double cream. Heat this mixture in a pan for a few hours on minimum heat, until a skin forms. Do not stir! Leave the pan in a cool place overnight, and the next day scoop off the lumpy cream from the surface. Discard the rest of the milk or use it for another purpose.

Scones: Don't bother fiddling around for too long. *Pengenna Pasties* (High Street) sell a special mixture – your scones will then taste like ones from your favourite baker.

CAFÉS
Traditional tearoom gossip
Bumbles Tearoom

Cornish cream teas, home-made cakes and scones, also hearty snacks such as baked potatoes and sandwiches.	**What?**
Because it's exactly what we expect of Cornwall. Time seems to be standing still here – in your mind's eye you can see your grandmother elegantly sipping her tea at one of the heavy circular wooden tables.	**Why?**
Daily 10am–5pm.	**When?**
The Digey, on the corner of Back Road West (nearly on Porthmeor Beach).	**Where?**

So close to the sea
Pedn-Olva Hotel

Is actually a hotel, but the café and restaurant are also open to non-residents. Good coffee.	**What?**
Because you couldn't be nearer the sea. The hotel is built into the cliff on the site of a former mine, and has a wonderful terrace and roof terrace with panoramic views of the whole of St Ives Bay. Also lovely inside – big glazed frontage, the perfect view from wherever you're sitting, comfy sofas.	**Why?**
Open from 10am–11pm. Bar snacks 12–6pm, dinner from 6.30pm–8.45pm. Tea and coffee all day long.	**When?**
The Warren, by Porthminster Beach, www.smalland friendly.co.uk.	**Where?**

Light and space
Porthminster Café

What? This historic place opened as a café two years before the Second World War, closed at the beginning of the war, and after the war deckchairs were mended here until 1990. Now you can once again enjoy the sea view and the flood of sunlight whilst eating and drinking. The food is extremely good, but it is also pretty expensive.

Why? Because life can be so relaxed. Purism meets comfort, plus a fantastic view of the whole of St Ives Bay as far as Godrevy Lighthouse.

When? In summer lunch from 12–4pm, afternoon tea, evening meals from 6.30pm. Now open all year round. Often hard to get a table – always make a reservation for evenings, and for weekends ideally two to three days in advance.

Where? Right on Porthminster Beach, Tel. 01736-795352, www.porthminstercafe.co.uk.

Reading matter
Tregenna Place Coffee Shop

Coffee, tea and delicious scones amidst shelves full of second-hand books to browse through in a former telephone exchange.

What?

Because the combination of books and hot drinks is inspiring. Right in the middle of town, yet all bustle remains outside. You don't get the feeling here that you must either order something else or leave.

Why?

Mon–Sat 10am–5pm.

When?

Tregenna Place. Easy to miss, as the entrance is hidden in an unprepossessing alley between two buildings. Go up the stairs.

Where?

Bird's-eye view
Tate Café

Everything and nothing – modest breakfast selection, sizeable lunch menu, coffee and delicious cakes. You can go to the Tate Gallery's café without visiting the gallery itself and without paying any entrance fee.

What?

Because it's sometimes nice to get on top of things. High up above the roofs of St Ives you can enjoy a unique and undistorted view of the old town and Porthmeor Beach.

Why?

March–October: Daily 10am–5.20pm, November–February: Tue–Sun 10am–4.20pm.

When?

In the Tate Gallery, right over Porthmeor Beach.

Where?

ICE CREAM
Straight from the farm
Kelly's Ice Cream

What?   Prize-winning ice cream, made since 1900 on a farm in Cornwall, using clotted cream.

Why?   Because fans of *Cadbury's Crunchie* will love the honeycomb ice. Common-or-garden vanilla ice and strawberry ice with real strawberries are also particularly good.

When?   Every day 10am–10pm.

Where?   The Wharf.

CONFECTIONERS AND FUDGE

Tip   Just follow your nose and press it against the numerous shop windows. There are confectioners offering delicious confectionery from Tregenna Place down High Street and along Fore Street, and fudge shops above all in Fore Street and along the harbour.

FROM A PERSONAL COOKBOOK
Grant Nethercott, owner and head chef of the **gourmet restaurant Alba**, grants us a recipe:

Warm chocolate tart with clotted cream

Rich shortcrust pastry:
170 g flour (plain)
100 g unsalted butter
pinch salt
1 egg yolk
tbsp. water

Chocolate filling:
300 g bitter chocolate
100 g unsalted butter
100 g castor sugar
100 ml double cream
4 whole eggs
4 egg yolks

Make the pastry in the normal way. Line an 8 inch flan dish with the pastry and blind bake for 10 minutes at 245 °C.
Place chocolate, butter, sugar and cream in a dish and melt slowly over a pot of hot water, when melted add the eggs and the yolks and beat until all the egg is incorporated.
Place the chocolate mix in the flan dish over the pastry and bake for 15–25 minutes at 245–260 °C. The chocolate should soufflé up when cooked and then sink back down as it cools to give a rich dense chocolate tart. Dust with cocoa or icing sugar and serve with clotted cream.

Alba Restaurant
Old Lifeboat House
Wharf Road
Tel. 01736-797222
www.thealbarestaurant.com

SHOPPING FOR FOOD

Fish   *Fresh, fresher...*
     ... Matthew Stevens & Son

What?   Wide range of the finest fresh fish and seafood from nearby harbours and St Ives itself. This family company, in its third generation, supplies delis, pubs und Michelin starred restaurants throughout Great Britain.

Why?   Because fresh fish should not smell fishy, but should only – as at Matthew Stevens – have a mild and pleasant sea aroma. And the presentation couldn't possibly be more appealing.

When?   Mon–Fri 8am–5pm, Sat 8am–12pm.

Where?   Back Road East, www.mstevensandson.co.uk.

Meat   **John B. Curnow & Sons:** Butcher selling the best sausages in the world. Pork & leek are our favourite. 60 Fore Street.

Fruit & vegetables   **The Floral Shop:** Big range of fresh fruit, vegetables and flowers. Mon–Sat 9am–5pm. Tregenna Hill/corner of Dove Street.
     Fore Street Deli: See under delis.

Supermarkets   **3 Co-ops:** 13–14 Tregenna Place and Royal Square (both Mon–Sat 8am–11pm, Sun 8am–10.30pm), and The Stennack.
     Costcutter in Carbis Bay: Mon–Sun 7am–10pm, St Ives Road.
     Tesco: A bit cheaper than the town centre grocers. Mon–Sat 8am–8pm, Sun 10am–4pm. On the way from St Ives to Carbis Bay – turn right at the roundabout, St Ives Road.

Norway Stores: Typical little corner shop with moderate prices for anyone staying in the *Downalong* area who happens to need milk or loo rolls. Back Road West.

McColls: Like a big petrol-station shop, selling sweets, snacks and magazines, and above all alcohol. Mon–Sun 7am–10pm, Tregenna Place.

Every Friday 9am-2.30pm in the Parish Rooms, St Andrews Street.

Farmers' market

DELIS

The fact that in St Ives one deli after another is opening shows once again that this little town is in every respect on its way to becoming a temple of Epicureanism – or maybe it already is. The following three delis are all well worth a visit:

First-class
Fore Street Deli

Big selection of fresh Cornish products, e.g. cheese, honey, beer, fruit and vegetables. Also delicious home-made cakes and pastries such as apricot muesli bars, the obligatory scones, goat's cheese tartlets and much more. Special service: welcome packs to be ordered in advance, containing everything you need at the beginning of your stay – delivered straight to your holiday accommodation.

What?

Because the deli has an outstanding in-house chef and baker.

Why?

| When? | During the season every day from 8am to about 10pm; in winter Mon–Sat 8am–6pm and Sun 10am–4.30pm. |
| Where? | 30A Fore Street, Tel. 01736-794578. |

Good service still on the menu

Deli Café

'Everything is possible' is the philosophy of this small but excellent deli/café/restaurant. If you want something special for breakfast Anna or Mark Ellwood will run to the shop round the corner. They also do outside deliveries to homes and hotels, and will knock up a beach picnic in a trice.

What?	Choice products from Cornwall and the West counties plus delicacies from all over the world to take away or eat in. Special recommendation: the baguettes, freshly baked every day, with tasty fillings such as roast beef, hummus, grilled pepper, rocket or horseradish (and you can compose your own fillings).
Why?	Because the bacon is fried in honey and you can choose the cheese for your cheeseburger from the deli counter. The small café area with just five wrought-iron tables creates a mixture of intimacy and cosmopolitan flair.
When?	In summer 7 days 9am–5pm, in winter Mon–Sat 9am–4pm. Breakfast until 12pm (sometimes later).
How much?	Main dishes £4.50 to £9.75.
Where?	3 Chapel Street, Tel. 01736-795100, www.cornish deli.com.

Piquancy and a feeling of wellbeing

The Digey Food Room

Specialities from Cornwall, Spain and Italy. Little delicacies to eat on the spot, breakfast, all-day lunch and coffee and cakes. The smoked fish is particularly tasty.   What?

Good food at reasonable prices, a cosy café and various (Cornish) magazines to look through.   Why?

In the summer every day from about 10.30am to 6pm, in winter Tue–Sat 10.30am–5pm, Sun 11am–4pm.   When?

4/6 The Digey, Tel. 01736-799600.   Where?

Culture

Entertainment

Arts Club

What?   Founded in 1890 as a community of professional artists, musicians and authors. The target group is now broader, and anyone interested in culture and wishing to promote art in all its forms of expression can become a member (provided they are proposed and seconded by a current member).

Wide range of performances, concerts, recitations and exhibitions, held on two storeys: downstairs the exhibition room and upstairs the stage and space for 60 seats. The building almost appears to be standing in the sea, and in stormy weather the waves can crash against, onto and even over the Arts Club, giving it a cosy yet eerie atmosphere.

Westcott's Quay, www.stivesartsclub.co.uk.   Where?

Events in the Arts Club (selection)

- **Kulture Brake: Cult comedy troupe** since 2002, and an **absolute must** for every visitor to St Ives fortunate enough to be there at the time of a show. **Chaotic and satirical** is the way the four very different characters – Rod Bullimore, Bernie Davies, Nicola Clark and Dhyano – present themselves. Variety atmosphere as a result of tables in the auditorium and BYO drinks.
- **Café Frug:** Open stage for poetry readings, musical offerings and sometimes a spontaneous combination of the two. Every second Thursday throughout the year with host Bob Devereux.
- **Bobdoq:** A surreal, novel mix of film, music, comedy and poetry by Dhyano and guests.
- **Club exhibition:** Twice a year (May and September) Arts Clubs members exhibit selected works, offering them for sale.

Kidz R Us

Ensemble made up of children and young people and   What?
offering high quality performances of shows and musicals, e.g. *Les Misérables*, *A Chorus Line* and *Jungle Book*. The 321-seat theatre was founded in 1994 to

promote young talent. Guest appearances at the *Palladium* and the *Royal Albert Hall* in London, and at the *Minack Theatre*.

Where? Lower Stennack, in the former Wesley Chapel next to the Backpackers Hostel, Tel. 01736-797007, www.kidzrus.net.

GHOST WALKS

Not just something for out-and-out tourists – these walks will give you the creeps and at the same time teach you something about the history of St Ives. The following is the more alternative and nicer of the (at least) two providers:

Lantern Ghost Storywalk

What? **Shanty Baba's** hour comes when the sun disappears behind the horizon and the shadows over the town grow longer. The born storyteller (and former tax advisor) conjures up ghosts, smugglers and other creatures of the night.

When? During the season three times a week (Wed/Thur/Sun) at 9pm. Look out for notices (in front of the Arts Club). Duration about 75 min.

Where? Starting point: Westcott's Quay next to the Arts Club, Tel. 07986-123305.

SEPTEMBER FESTIVAL

What? **Two-week 'state of alert' in St Ives**. Live music can be heard in every pub, poets recite on the streets, artists open up their studios, and music emanates from the church. Alongside jazz legends and best-selling authors there remains room for experiments involving lesser-known artists and for anyone simply wanting to give it a go.

The festival was founded in 1978 by a group of idealists in order to bring to St Ives national and international representatives of various art forms, and not least to extend the holiday season in the town. A Fringe Festival also developed over the years alongside the actual event. This was an alternative auxiliary programme organised independently by ambitious artists, which in 2003 and 2004 even took place as an event in its own right. Today, under the management of the *St Ives September Fringe Festival Committee*, the festival is unique in the scope of its offering. The programme encompasses **classical music, folk, jazz, blues, rock, world music, poetry, readings, theatre, comedy, cabaret, lectures, film screenings, open studios and art exhibitions.** For the past two years Tate St Ives has also offered a series of classical concerts and other events as part of the festival. The *Lifeboat Inn* provides its own simultaneous fringe festival of live music. Early booking of accommodation advised!

When? Annually in the second and third week of September (Saturday to Saturday inclusive).

Where? Information at www.stivesseptemberfestival.co.uk and from Martin Val Baker (founder member in 1978 and one of the current organisers) on Tel. 01736-366077, info@rainydaygallery.co.uk.

NEW YEAR'S EVE

On the final night of the year St Ives wakes up from its hibernation and celebrates. The place becomes one big party – in all the pubs, bars and restaurants and above all **in the streets people celebrate and dance**, throwing all inhibitions overboard. And **everyone is in fancy dress**! If you don't like huge gatherings then stay away. Book accommodation as soon as possible.

Then as now: St Ives is Art and Art is St Ives

In every corner of the little harbour town you'll find a gallery, a studio, an artist or at least artistic subject matter. In 1811 the great **J. M. W. Turner** was the first person to sketch the picturesque harbour view over the rooftops of St Ives. In 1883/84 the American painter James Whistler and his pupil Walter Sickert spent the winter here, attracted by the diverse subject matter – above all the still famous **Mediterranean light** of St Ives. Artists now came to the fishing village in their hordes, resulting in the founding of two important and still existing establishments: the **Arts Club** in 1890 and the **St Ives Society of Artists** in 1927.

The artists' colony was given fresh and indeed crucial impetus by three events:

- The arrival of the **master potter Bernard Leach**, who moved from Asia and settled in St Ives in 1920.

- The 1938 founding of the **St Ives School of Painting** by Leonard Fuller and his wife Marjorie Mostyn.
- The arrival at the outbreak of WW2 of an influential group of artists from Hampstead, including **Ben Nicholson**, **Barbara Hepworth** and the Russian artist **Naum Gabo**.

Abstraction rules! Different worlds suddenly clashed in the little town, which had hitherto been a hive of artistic activity but which adhered to traditional and objective forms of expression. British marine tradition, Japanese philosophy, Russian constructivism and the awareness of French style such as true naive art – worlds which did not compete with each other but gave rise to mutual stimulation, joint experimentation and the creation of new approaches.

1949 saw the founding of the **Penwith Society of Artists**, a group which splintered off because of growing tensions within the more traditional *St Ives Society of Artists*. The founder members – all of them champions of abstraction – included Hepworth, Nicholson and Leach.

From the mid-40s to the 60s St Ives and New York were the two most important artists' colonies in the world.

St Ives-based artists

Barbara Hepworth (1903–1975): She and Henry Moore are the most important sculptors of the 20th century. Hepworth, Moore and Naum Gabo developed the concept of non-representational sculpture. Her sculptures in marble, wood and bronze reflect natural shapes.

Ben Nicholson (1894–1982): Hepworth's husband, who was much influenced by Picasso and Mondrian. The latter coined the term neoplasticism, a concept that became crucial to Nicholson's works, i.e. an emphasis on verticals and horizontals and the primary colours yellow, red and blue.

Alfred Wallis (1855–1942): As a 70-year-old ex-mariner Wallis started painting (ship paint on wooden planks) unnoticed in his cottage in *Downalong*, and in 1928 he was discovered and furthered by Nicholson, who was impressed by his naivety and his assured style.

Naum Gabo (1890–1977): Russian Bauhaus teacher and constructivist who came to St Ives in 1939. Simple geometric forms and a belief in modern technology were more important to Gabo than decorative considerations. His metal/glass/plastic creations were ground breaking for modern sculpture.

Bernard Leach (1887–1979): Spent eleven years studying the craft of pottery in Asia. He came to St Ives in 1920 and together with the Japanese ceramicist Shoiji Hamada founded the Leach Pottery, where he combined western subject matter with oriental elements.

Patrick Heron (1920–1999): Briefly a pupil of Leach. Worked in St Andrews Street for seven years. His style is characterised by generous use of colour, which almost seems to run down the canvas. The huge glass window mosaic in the Tate Gallery foyer is his last great work.

TATE ST IVES AND HEPWORTH MUSEUM
Tate St Ives

One of the four Tate galleries, the others being Tate Modern and Tate Britain in London and Tate Liverpool. Tate St Ives was **opened in 1993 by Prince Charles**, and shows modern art in a Cornish context. The gallery's own collection comprises works by all the relevant artists who have worked in St Ives. What makes Tate St Ives so attractive is probably the almost magical relationship between its dynamic architecture, its mighty surroundings and its exhibits, which reflect this interplay. The gallery has an **enormous influence on tourism** (and unfortunately on traffic in the town). Changing exhibitions of national and international contemporary art and ceramics, regular courses, workshops, lectures and concerts take place.

What?

When?	March–October: Mon–Sun 10am–5.20pm, entry until 5pm. November–February: Tue–Sun 10am–4.20pm, entry until 4pm.
How much?	£5.75 for adults, reductions £3.25, free entry for the under 18s and over 60s. (Tate and Hepworth Museum with a combined ticket cheaper than with single tickets.)
Where?	Right on Porthmeor Beach, www.tate.org.uk/stives.

Barbara Hepworth Museum & Sculpture Garden

What?	Barbara Hepworth's studio and sculpture garden, where she lived and worked from 1949 onwards until her death in 1975 as a result of a fire in her studio. You can now view her sculptures, paintings, drawings, private photos and letters here. Her **workshops have been left exactly as they were**, and the tools, overalls and half-worked stones lying around give the impression that Hepworth has just left the room for a moment. Hepworth's sculpture garden, in which she personally positioned most of her bronze sculptures amidst tropical plants, is an **oasis of calm** (provided there aren't too many visitors).
When?	Same opening hours as Tate St Ives.
How much?	£4.75 for adults, reductions £2.75, free entry for the under 18s and over 60s.
Where?	Barnoon Hill, www.tate.org.uk/stives/hepworth.

GALLERIES
Wills Lane Gallery

What?	Over the years this tiny gallery, which opened in 1968, has exhibited all the important contemporary artists associated with St Ives and Cornwall. The owner is the

architect Henry C. Gilbert, a close friend of Barbara
Hepworth and a real specialist in 20th-century art.
Wills Lane (a few metres from Market Place).   Where?

Salthouse Gallery
All-round gallery run by the all-round artist Bob De-   What?
vereux, who has expanded his gallery of abstract art
to create a **showplace for first-class events**. Poetry
readings and musical events take place here regularly.
During the September Festival the adjacent Norway
Square is an open stage for spontaneous performances every lunchtime from 12.30pm.
Norway Square.   Where?

**Bob Devereux's top five
St Ives galleries:**
- New Millennium Gallery
- Belgrave Gallery
- Plumbline Gallery
- Wills Lane Gallery
- Salthouse Gallery

Bob Devereux – painter, poet, librettist and giant of the 'scene'
– came to St Ives over 40 years ago, attracted by the creative,
innovative energy of the colony of abstract artists. 'The colony
began to fade at the point when I arrived,' says Bob with a wink.
He took over the Salthouse Gallery in 1979.

Penwith Gallery
Home of the **Penwith Society of Artists**, a society   What?
of **abstract artists** founded in 1949. The building

in *Downalong* – a former pilchard cellar – is now an imposing complex of galleries, studios and printers' workshops.

Where?   Back Road West.

Mariners Gallery

What?   Since 1945 this former church (The Mariners Church) has been the exhibition space for the works of the **St Ives Society of Artists**. Unlike the *Penwith Society*, the Society of Artists in particular promotes and shows **representational art**.

Where?   Norway Square, www.stivessocietyofartists.com.

Belgrave Gallery

What?   Since its opening in 1998 one of the leading galleries for the *St Ives modernist period* (late 30s to early 60s). In addition to an extensive stock of works from this period it especially shows works by contemporary artists.

Where?   22 Fore Street, www.belgravegallery.com.

New Millennium Gallery

What?   **Biggest private gallery** in St Ives. It was founded in 1996 and rapidly became one of the top galleries – and not just in the context of local/regional art. Displays works both by leading artists from St Ives and by nationally renowned artists working in West Cornwall, to whom solo exhibitions can be devoted thanks to the spaciousness of the gallery (on three storeys). The focus is on innovative, contemporary, abstract art.

Where?   Street-an-Pol, opposite the Tourist Information Centre, www.newmillenniumgallery.co.uk.

Plumbline Gallery

This gallery, founded in 1994, is Cornwall's only gallery specialising in contemporary national and international **glass art**.

2 Barnoon Hill, opposite Barbara Hepworth Museum.

What?

Where?

The Good-Mood Gallery

'It's fun!' – in conversation with **gallery owner Paul Vibert**

Definitely not one of the run-of-the-mill galleries in St Ives. **Creative chaos** sums it up. You have to rummage through piles of unframed pictures on tables and on the floor. The owner, Paul Vibert, has an overview, as well as a **completely different concept from that of most gallery owners**. He is primarily a collector, which means all of his pictures belong to him before he sells them.

'Because I buy things I have to like them,' says Paul. The style of the works he exhibits is **'somewhat bizarre, colourful and figurative, concentrating on feelings, slightly naive but often not, and provocative'**. His gallery houses works by about 25 artists – mostly from St Ives or its environs. The works often reside in his gallery before being exhibited elsewhere.

Externally The Gallery is pretty unprepossessing. *'I don't do any advertising, because I undercut other galleries,'* says Paul. *'I'm more for a discreet approach, and I sometimes sell things for a fiver less than the purchase price if I notice that someone really wants a picture but can't afford it – but it's not a charity shop!'*

The Gallery

Street-an-Pol (opposite the Guildhall)

CRAFTWORK
Leach Pottery

What? The workshop of the famous potter Bernard Leach and the museum dedicated to him are **in a state of flux.** In 2006 Penwith District Council bought this historic site, and it is now (status 03/2007) thoroughly renovating the premises. Soon, not only will visitors be able to view original pieces by the master and see the first oriental climbing kiln in the western hemisphere but **students and craftsmen will be working here again.** One of Leach's pupils, Trevor Corser, worked here for 35 years (until 2005).

When? **Re-opening scheduled for October 2007.** Enquiries to appeal@leachproject.co.uk.

Where? Higher Stennack (on the main road to Zennor), www.leachpottery.com, www.leachproject.co.uk.

Sloop Craft Market

What? In 1969 the much-imitated Sloop Craft Market was the first of its kind in the whole of Great Britain. The new concept was to accommodate several craftsmen in small, separate stone units and thus put everything under one roof. To this day you can peer over the shoulders of woodcarvers, goldsmiths, ceramicists and other craftsmen as they work.

Where? Slightly concealed, right behind the *Sloop Inn.*

New Craftsman Gallery and Craft Shop

What? Janet Leach, wife of Bernard Leach, opened the gallery in the 60s. Shortly afterwards she was joined by Mary Redgrave, whose children are the current owners. It used to be one of the first galleries specialising in contemporary Cornish art and ceramics. It now also

sells jewellery and other craftwork.
24 Fore Street, www.newcraftsmanstives.com.   Where?

fish pye pottery

In 1994 Laura McCrossen opened her little pottery in   What?
Downalong, and in 1994 and 1995 she **designed soap
dishes and beakers for Habitat.** She mainly works in
stoneware, earthenware and terracotta, often using
nautical themes. Cafés and restaurants all over St Ives
have her sugar bowls and flower vases on their tables.
Look out for the logo, a stylised fishbone! Also wall
panels, tiles, sculptures and pottery by Bob Wilcox.
47 Back Road East (corner of Porthmeor Road).   Where?

STUDIOS
Open Studios Day

As early as in 1910, in his book *Days in Cornwall*, C.   What?
Hind Lewis mentioned 80 studios in *Downalong*. They
were opened to the public once a year, and special excursions to St Ives were organised for these openings.
These *Show Days* ceased in the 50s, but the tradition
has recently been revived in the form of an Open Studios Day during the September Festival. 2006 saw the
involvement of 37 artists, whose work is usually only
to be seen as finished exhibits.

Map of participating studios available from the *St Ives*   Where?
Times & Echo's shop, High Street, and on the back of
the festival programme. Many, but not all of the studios are in the old fishing quarter, including the famous *Porthmeor Studios* and the *Sail Loft Studios*.

Porthmeor Studios

What?   For a century the present Porthmeor Studios were the **heart of the fishing industry**. This is where the pilchards were stacked up, and then salted and pressed in a huge basin to remove liquid and facilitate preservation. In 1886 the upper storey – the net lofts – was turned into artists' studios, and has since been **one of the main workplaces for the most important local artists**. Four of the cellars, incidentally, are still used by the fishermen of St Ives.

Where? Back Road West.

SCHOOL OF PAINTING
The St Ives School of Painting

What?   The school started in 1938 and attracted painters from all over the world. It now offers a large number of different courses for all age groups and levels all year round. The weekly life classes, which have now been going for 30 years, have become an institution. Beginners welcome!

Where? Back Road West (*Porthmeor Studios*), opposite Norway Square. Programme at www.stivesartschool.co.uk or Tel. 01736 797180.

Literature

LIBRARY
St Ives Library
Well-equipped library and the **best Internet option** in town. The first half hour is always free. The interior of the 1897 building was totally renovated in 2006. You will also find works by local artists here, e. g. Hepworth, Nicholson, Barns-Graham und Smart.   *What?*

Tue 9.30am–9.30pm, Wed–Fri 9.30am–8pm (in winter until 6pm), Sat 9.30am–12.30pm, Sun and Mon closed.   *When?*

Gabriel Street, www.cornwall.gov.uk/library.   *Where?*

BOOKSHOPS
St Ives Bookshop
Small bookshop with pleasant atmosphere and wide selection. Many books are signed (though no more expensive). Very friendly service.   *What?*

2 Fore Street.   *Where?*

The Harbour Bookshop
Biggest bookshop in St Ives. Huge selection of publications on Cornwall and books by local authors, but also everything else you expect from a good bookshop. Expert advice.   *What?*

Tregenna Place.   *Where?*

The Harbour Bookshop Too
Specialises in children's books, postcards and various bargains.   *What?*

Tregenna Place, directly opposite the other *Harbour Bookshop*.   *Where?*

Tate Bookshop

What? Art books as far as the eye can see. A lot about Cornish artists, but certainly not exclusively. Also literature on St Ives and the region. The Tate Gallery also has its own publishing house *(Tate Publishing)*, one of the leading publishers in the field of visual art.

Where? At Tate St Ives, Porthmeor Beach.

Tregenna Place Second Hand Books

What? Cosy café and second-hand bookshop in one. Big range of thematically arranged and inexpensive reading material. Anyone who loves books can become totally absorbed here.

Where? Tregenna Place – the entrance is easy to miss.

St Ives Times & Echo

What? St Ives' only weekly newspaper is published by the *St Ives Printing & Publishing Company*, which also brings out many books on St Ives and Cornish topics.

Where? High Street – entrance between *Boots* and *HSBC Bank*.

The Book Gallery

What? Books and art. Specialises in everything to do with the artists' colony: manuscripts, letters, catalogues, drawings, prints, magazines and much more. Book lists are compiled in accordance with customers' specific wishes.

Where? Chapel Street.

LITERATURE FESTIVAL

Bob Devereux *(Salthouse Gallery)* is planning to set up an annual literature festival, probably starting in May 2007. Just pop into his gallery and ask, or Tel. 01736-795003.

LITERARY ACCOMMODATION
Talland House

Up to the age of twelve Virginia Woolf spent her summer holidays on this grand late-Victorian estate. **Six smart holiday apartments** with fabulous views of Godrevy Lighthouse – the source of inspiration for her novel *To the Lighthouse* – are now located here. Woolf's father, Sir Leslie Stephen, was at the time active in local art and literature circles.

What?

From £110 to £950 a week depending on size and time of year.

How much?

Talland Road, Tel. 01736-755050, www.tallandhouse.com.

Where?

NOVELS SET IN ST IVES AND ITS ENVIRONS

- **Virginia Woolf:** *To the Lighthouse* (first published 1927): Autobiographically influenced novel in which Woolf processes her childhood memories. The focus of the story is Godrevy Lighthouse, near St Ives, though the novel is actually set in Scotland.
- **D. H. Lawrence:** *Women in Love* (first published 1921): Deemed to be the author's masterpiece. In 1916 Lawrence and his German wife Frieda moved to Zennor, where he was unable to live the peaceful life far from the war that he had expected; he was even suspected of espionage. This was where he wrote parts of *Women in Love*, at the time a controversial novel, and full of gloomy visions of humanity.
- **Daphne du Maurier novels:** Not actually set in the immediate vicinity of St Ives, but thoroughly deserve a mention, as du Maurier, unlike any other author, knows how to intertwine Cornwall's raw and mystical landscape with her exciting stories. *Jamaica Inn* (1936) und *Rebecca* (1940) are particularly recommendable.
- **Marion Whybrow:** *Shadow over Summer* (2004): Set in central St Ives, with high recognition value of the settings. An author rents *Talland House* so as to immerse herself in the atmosphere that inspired Virginia Woolf. Whybrow has lived in St Ives since 1980.
- **Helen Dunmore:** *Zennor in Darkness* (1994): Skilled interlinking of fact and fiction. During WW1 a young girl ends up in Zennor and comes under the influence of the mysterious author D. H. Lawrence.
- **Rosamunde Pilcher novels:** The fictitious little town of Porthkerries, in which many of the Pilcher novels are set (especially *The Shell Seekers*), is actually St Ives. The author, born just round the corner in Lelant in 1924, depicts with great attention to detail the little fishing community with its alleys and beaches. The establishment she calls 'Castle Hotel' is in reality the venerable hotel *Tregenna Castle*. Over 30 million Pilcher books have hitherto been sold worldwide.

NON-FICTION ON ST IVES-RELATED TOPICS

- **Henry C. Gilbert/Roy Ray/Colin Orchard:** *Art about St Ives* (2006): Very up-to-date and compulsory reading for anyone interested in art in St Ives. Presentations of many galleries, studios and historic sites, with photos and short texts that make good reading. The little book is also visually pleasing.

- **Marion Whybrow:** *St Ives 1893-1993. Portrait of an Art Colony* (2002): Comprehensive overall portrait of the founding of the Arts Club up to the founding of *Tate St Ives*, with over 300 illustrations. Further literature by Whybrow is available, on various topics related to the art of St Ives.

- **Tom Cross:** *Painting the Warmth of the Sun. St Ives Artists 1939–1975* (2006): The artists' colony and its effects on the art world.

- **Sue Lewington:** *A Day in St Ives* (2006): Actually more an artwork than a book. Beautiful illustrations from sunrise to sunset in St Ives, with high recognition value. A book to fall in love with.

- **Peter Stanier:** *St Ives Guide* (2004): Unlike the present, primarily practically oriented *goldfinch guide*, the Cornishman Stanier focuses on current and historical background information on all areas connected with St Ives. A good complement.

Music

LIVE MUSIC

When wandering around town on a summer evening it is hard to ignore the sound of guitars and singing emanating from various pubs. This is what makes St Ives so attractive: You go out with no fixed aim, pop your head in here and there, stay for a beer and a couple of songs and then continue on your expedition. Entry is always free. Main styles of music presented: jazz, blues, folk and rock. Outside the season – from after the September Festival (see chapter ‚Entertainment') until about Easter – Friday is the night of nights for live music. The main venues are as follows:

'The last jazz club before New York'
Western Hotel

What?	THE place for live music. The hotel has three bars – the Function Room, the Craic Bar and the Kettle 'n' Wink – and in the summer there is a band playing in at least one of them every night.
Where?	Royal Square, Tel. 01736-795277, www.westernhotel stives.co.uk.
How much?	Entry free, except for some events in the Function Room. £2.40–£2.90 a pint in all three bars.

Function Room

What?	The Western usually means the events room. This is on two levels, has a bar, seats 150 and now features a big screen (so that people sitting at the back can see what's going on). It is home to the **St Ives Jazz Club**. Every Tuesday the club, founded in 1998, presents

the very finest of performers on the contemporary modern jazz scene. The offering is an excellent mix of leading national and international artists and promising young musicians. The *St Ives Blues Club* also stages performances here.

Jazz Club: Tuesdays 9pm–11.15pm (with a break, doors from 8pm) throughout the year, Tel. 01736-798061, www.stivesjazzclub.com. Blues Club: usually the last Thursday of the month. Information on Tel. 01736-794608 (Guy). **When?**

Jazz Club: £8 non-members, £5 members. **How much?**

> *Oh Mother dear, I'm over here and I'm never coming back.*
> *What keeps me here is the Beer, the Women and the Craic.*

Craic Bar

What? Irish bar with a green interior. There are regular jam sessions, concerts and open mic nights here.

When? 7pm to midnight. Tue: Acoustic Session, i.e. a folk club. Wed: open mic (during the summer months), Sat: frequent blues concerts (acoustic).

Kettle 'n' Wink

What? The Western Hotel's third bar, which tends to be quieter than the Craic Bar. Open jam session every afternoon during the festival.

When? 11am to midnight. Concerts usually Fri (rockabilly, blues, jazz, rock).

Golden Lion

What? Traditional pub **concentrating on rock music** right in the heart of St Ives. Quiet lounge bar at the front, and music bar at the back. Fridays loud rock music (incl. indie, punk, rock'n'roll), Sundays often acoustic and/ or folk. On Saturdays there is now a kind of disco with music videos on a big screen. On Sundays many locals meet here at lunchtime to play cards.

When? Daily 11am to midnight. Concerts Fri and Sun throughout the year; Sat: music video disco.

Where? Tel. 01736-793679, Market Place.

In discussion with
Martyn Barker (from Yorkshire).
A **musician** who has been coming to St Ives for ten years – always to the September Festival (and at Easter and ...), above all because of the music.

'There's a huge choice of music. You can see so many different acts here in a single evening, involving greatly differing styles and instruments. And not just during the festival. An incredible number of songwriters live here, which is very inspiring and attracts musicians from all over the world.'

Percussion or fiddle? Fiddle.
Inside or outside? Outside, especially in Norway Square every lunchtime during the festival.
Acoustic or electronic? Acoustic.
Blues or jazz? Blues.
Jazz or punk? Jazz.
Lager or ale? Ale.
Beer or wine? Both.

Lifeboat Inn
Big harbour pub in a former auction house, which **runs its own fringe festival during the September Festival**. Also good food all day long.   What?
Sun: always live music during the day – currently 3–5pm. Fri: concerts (many genres).   When?
Tel. 01736-794123, Wharf Road.   Where?

Queens Hotel

What? A lot of music, primarily jazz and blues. Jam session every Wednesday with the master of instruments Joey Gillard, who invites budding musicians onto the stage with him.

When? Wed: jam session, Fri: often concerts.

Where? Tel. 01736-796468, High Street.

CLASSICAL MUSIC

St Ives is not exactly a mecca for classical music, but the little there is, is of the highest standard.

St Ia Church

What? The **International Musicians Seminar** (IMS) puts on one concert in the Parish Church of St Ia in the spring (usually April) and one in September. The IMS operates from nearby Prussia Cove, a former smugglers' haunt. It was founded in 1972, and twice a year top musicians from various countries come to courses and play together. Chamber music for strings and piano is the standard fare. At the end of May there is also the charity series **Music in May**, usually comprising music for strings, piano and clarinet. The September Festival programmes classical concerts in the church, and there are also occasional one-off performances there.

Where? Market Place. IMS tickets on Tel. 01736-731688, or visit www.i-m-s.org.uk. www.stivesseptemberfestival. co.uk. *Music in May:* Andrew Moth, Tel. 01736-798433.

Western Hotel

Occasional classical concerts in the Function Room.

Tate St Ives/Hepworth Sculpture Garden

Tate St Ives puts on classical concerts from time to time, both in the Tate and the Hepworth Sculpture Garden – especially during the September Festival. It also has an occasional series called *Late at Tate*.

CINEMA

Royal Cinema

St Ives boasts a cinema with three screens. It usually shows current blockbusters, and about once a week the Penwith Film Society, a non-profit organisation, screens alternative films – usually foreign ones (not during the summer months).

What?

Royal Square, Tel. 01736-796843, www.merlincinemas.co.uk, www.penwithfilmsociety.co.uk.

Where?

Adults £5.50, children and pensioners £3.50.

How much?

Cinema magazine

Movie Magic is the magazine of the Cornwall/Devon cinema chain *Merlin Cinemas*, to which the *Royal Cinema* in St Ives belongs. For a typically commercial in-house magazine, *Movie Magic* shows tangible enthusiasm. There is an emphasis on the editorial section, and it includes a good events calendar for Cornwall, weighted towards music (with St Ives as a separate sub heading).

What?

Available in the cinema or at www.cornwallmoviemagic.co.uk.

Where?

Free of charge.

How much?

ST IVES AS A FILM LOCATION

Nearly everyone ambling through St Ives will at least once think 'What a location!' And it's hardly surprising that countless directors have also had this very thought and have selected St Ives and its environs as a setting for their films.

- **Raise the Titanic** (1980): With Alec Guinness. Locations include the *Sloop Inn*. But the film flopped as a result of various setbacks. For example, a $ 350,000 model of the Titanic was made that was too big for the tank in which it was to be filmed. Finally a new, larger tank was built for a cool $ 6m.
- **To the Lighthouse** (1983): BBC TV film after the eponymous book by Virginia Woolf. Family drama in the novel's original setting around Godrevy Lighthouse.
- **Blue Juice** (1994): Superficially a surfing film (aptly enough for St Ives), but actually a story about growing up. With Catherine Zeta-Jones.
- **Ladies in Lavender** (2005): A Polish refugee in the 30s who is shipwrecked on his way to New York and gets stranded in Cornwall. Beautiful landscape shots, with Oscar winners Maggie Smith und Judi Dench.

Rosamunde Pilcher locations

Every Sunday evening German households wonder: Shall we take a look at Cornwall today? Ever since 1993, week after week the German broadcasting company *ZDF* has been transmitting its own filmings of the novels by the best-selling author Rosamunde Pilcher, who was born in Lelant. It is only through this TV series that many Germans know about the spectacular Cornish coast, the idyllic fishing villages, the deserted bays, the imposing country houses and the exotic gardens. Many of the films are set in St Ives and its surroundings, since in Rosamunde Pilcher's novels the town serves as a basis for her fictitious village of Porthkerries. The German films have been sold to 28 countries – a fact that has greatly boosted tourism in Cornwall and continues to do so.

In 2002 Rosamunde Pilcher even received the British Tourist Award for her contribution to tourism.

Some of the locations for the Pilcher films:

- **Porthminster Café:** The café scenes for *Voices in Summer* and *The Empty House* were filmed here. It is also where the crew hold their post-shoot parties. On Porthminster Beach.

- **Tregenna Castle:** The castle-like hotel in the film *Another View* is called the 'Castle Hotel', and Rosamunde Pilcher actually used *Tregenna Castle* as a model in her novels. The 18th-century-style building is covered with wild vines and is located above the road to Carbis Bay.

- **Sloop Inn:** In her books Pilcher calls the quaint fishermen's and artists' pub on the harbour 'Sliding Tackle'. *Another View* was filmed here.

- **Lelant:** Untypical combination – the golf course used for filming is right next to the 15th century church of St Uny, where the River Hayle flows into St Ives Bay. A fateful exchange of words takes place here in *Voices in Summer*.

- **St Erth Station:** Backdrop for moving farewell scenes, mostly involving female main characters. In reality the little railway station admittedly looks far less attractive than in the films, but the train journey from St Erth to St Ives is extremely worthwhile.

- **Zennor:** The home of Celtic myths and sagas provides the setting for the films *The Empty House and Snow in April*.

- **Gurnard's Head:** The dreamy cottage called 'Bosithick' in *The Empty House* is a particularly romantic motif. This little house on the cliffs is actually a B&B called 'Cove Cottage'. Peninsular west of Zennor.

FILMS ABOUT ST IVES

A fair number of documentary-makers have taken a shine to St Ives and used it for a wide variety of topics. The *South West Film & Television Archive* in Plymouth houses around 110,000 films and video clips on all relevant topics in the southwest from the 20s to the present day. They include amusing little films by amateur film-makers about their own families on seaside holidays. Various clips, e.g. *Barbara Hepworth*, can be viewed on the website, other films can be ordered from the archive.

Information: www.movinghistory.ac.uk/archives/sw.

- **Untitled** (1932): Film about the St Ives Lifeboat, which was the last sailing ship of its kind. It sank a year after the film came out.
- **South Crofty Tin Mine** (1934): Major Gill on Europe's last working tin mine (near Camborne). Was shut down in 1998 and has been open to the public since 2003.
- **The Gem of the Cornish Riviera** (1938/39): Prize-winning film by the brothers John und William Barnes about life as a fisherman in St Ives.
- **St Ives in the 50s:** James Couch on the St Ives of the 50s. The film is regularly shown at the Arts Club during the September Festival.
- **Barbara Hepworth** (1968): TV documentary on the sculptor who lived and worked in St Ives, including interviews.
- **The Potter's Art** (1970): TV film about the life and work of the potter Bernard Leach, St Ives.
- **Painting the Warmth of the Sun** (1984): Three-part series on artists of the *St Ives School* and the *Newlyn School*, including interviews with the artists and with critics.

FILM MUSEUM
Barnes Museum of Cinemaphotography

Opened in 1963 under the management of John and Carmen Barnes, the museum showed the history of moving images from the 17th to the

20th century, for which the Barnes brothers had been collecting material for over 40 years. The museum was closed in 1986, but anyone interested can still view the collection by arrangement.
Information: Tel. 01736-794080.

Film websites

- **www.rosemarylinks.co.uk/film.htm**: Broad overview of (TV) films set in Cornwall.
- **www.cornwallfilmfestival.com**: Since November 2002 annual festival in Falmouth on Cornish topics and Cornish film-makers.
- **www.cornwallfilm.com**: Insider site for film-makers who choose Cornwall as a location. Information on production companies, locations and the wealth of (financial) support available.

Sights

St Ives Parish Church

Christians have prayed here for over 1,000 years. The current building dates from 1426, and the granite for the tower was shipped in from Zennor. The base of the tower may well be part of a still older church. The interior of the church reflects various periods. The pew ends, for example, are decorated with typical 15th century Cornish carvings, and the chancel panelling dates from the Jacobean period (early 17th century). The statue next to the cross depicts the patron saint Ia, from whom St Ives takes its name. To the right of the altar, in the *Lady Chapel*, is Hepworth's marble sculpture *Madonna and Child* (1954). Market Place, www.saint-ives.org.

Market Place

The market place is not a square but a round granite building dating from 1832. Until 1940 the town council was accommodated here before moving into the Guildhall.

1 Tate Gallery
2 Barbara Hepworth Museum
  and Sculpture Garden
3 Leach Pottery
4 St Ives Museum
5 Archive
6 Parish Church
7 Market Place
8 Trewyn Gardens
9 Lifeboat station
10 Catholic Church
11 The Malakoff
12 St Leonard's Chapel
13 St Nicolas' Chapel
14 Battery
15 Barnoon Cemetery

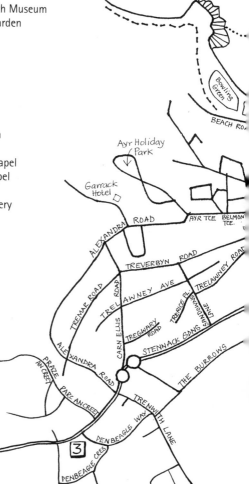

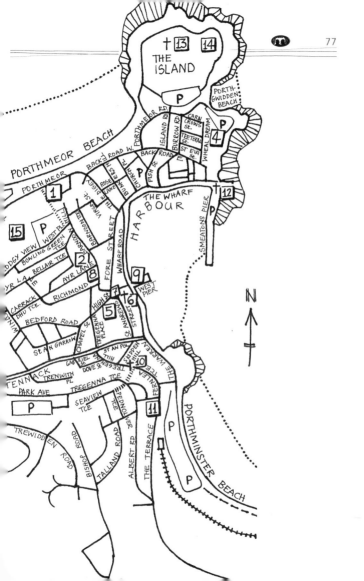

Trewyn Gardens

Although only a few metres from the main shopping street, this beautiful park with its subtropical plants (which flourish in the mild Cornish climate) is somewhat hidden away. You can sit on a bench here and eat your lunch in peace and quiet – and well away from greedy gulls. Here you will also find the sculpture *Megalith II* (1974) by John Milne, a pupil of Hepworth, in whose memory he donated the sculpture to the town. Between Back Street und Ayr Lane.

Lifeboat

In 1840 the *Hope* was the first lifeboat in St Ives. The present lifeboat, *The Princess Royal*, is kept in a special building erected in 1994 on the West Pier. The former lifeboat station now houses *Alba* – a restaurant named after the eponymous steamship. In 1938 the *Alba* was shipwrecked on Porthmeor Beach, and at very low tide you can still make out parts of the bow and the boiler near the rocks of The Island. For visitors it is always a spectacle when the **lifeboat is towed into the sea by a tractor** – a regular occurrence for practice purposes.

Church of the Sacred Heart and St Ia

The Catholic church was built in 1909, and contains a picture by Leonard J. Fuller, the founder of the *St Ives School of Painting*. The church is open to visitors after mass on Sundays. Tregenna Hill.

The Malakoff

The view of the town and the harbour seen from The Malakoff forms the subject matter for many a photo and painting. This vantage point was named after the Battle of Malakoff, fought between the French und the Russians in 1855, because the square was built at this time and lads from St Ives used to play soldiers here. In 1972 a small garden was opened, in which Hepworth's bronze statue *Epidaurus II* (1961) now stands. Next to the bus station.

St Leonard's Chapel

For centuries fishermen prayed here before setting off to sea. **They paid the chaplain with fishes**, the quantity varying according to the catch. The chapel is now a memorial to the fishermen of St Ives. Quay Street, at the beginning of Smeaton's Pier.

St Nicholas' Chapel

St Nicholas was the patron saint of seafarers and children. The chapel was probably built in the early 15th century, and was the vantage point from which so-called 'Preventive Men' used to look out for smugglers. In 1904 St Nicholas' Chapel was almost completely destroyed by the Navy Office, who had used the chapel as a storage room. Reconstructed in 1911 and restored in 1971. During the season the chapel, which houses Bernard Leach's *Pilgrim Plate*, is open to visitors. The Island.

Smuggling – *a digression*

The majority of Cornish people are said to have been involved in the smuggling trade. According to records dating from 1598 pots, alcohol and salt (needed for preserving fish) were the chief items smuggled. It is to be assumed that **every pub in St Ives was involved in the illegal trade**, and that even the 'guards' were implicated. Smuggling was very lucrative, the inhabitants of St Ives being glad to be able to get certain luxury goods in town at attractive prices.

Battery
The Battery on the Island has three circular foundations for canons, and three guns were positioned there in 1887 to protect the harbour and Porthmeor Beach against enemies. The site of the easternmost canon later became the *National Coastwatch Institution*'s lookout platform. The Island, eastern end.

Barnoon Cemetery
Immediately above Porthmeor Beach, thus it probably has **one of the best views of any cemetery in the world**. The artist **Alfred Wallis** was buried here in 1942, and the ceramicist Bernard Leach decorated his grave with painted tiles. On the hill right behind Tate St Ives.

MUSEUM AND ARCHIVE
St Ives Museum

What?	The museum, founded back in 1924, covers all important topics relating to the history of St Ives und its environs, including fishing, mining, farming and seafaring. Many typical objects, photos and pictures are on display.
When?	Open from Easter to the end of October, Mon–Fri 10am–5pm, Sat 10am–4pm.
Where?	Wheal Dream, 75 metres from Smeaton's Pier. Follow signs from the harbour.

St Ives Trust Archive Study Centre

What?	Archive for the history of the town, including information on every conceivable topic relating to St Ives. Also films and over 10,000 photos (some copies for sale). Helpful staff on site.
When?	Tue–Fri 10.30am–5pm.
Where?	St Andrews Street. In the same building as the Parish Rooms, on the first floor. Entry through the little alley alongside *Powells Cottage Holidays*.

Media

St Ives Times & Echo: St Ives has its own weekly paper, which comes out on Fridays. Founded in 1889 and since 1951 in the hands of the Carver family. It's Toni Carver who prints the September Festival programme, which is appended to the paper as a supplement. 60p.

Newspaper

There's not yet a magazine dedicated to St Ives alone, but there are at least three for the whole of Cornwall. 'Inside Cornwall' is particularly recommendable:

Magazine

- **Inside Cornwall:** Glossy monthly magazine focusing on food, art, lifestyle, events and gardens. £2.50.

- **Pirate FM:** This is the only private radio station in Cornwall, and it has been transmitting since 1992. Music from the 70s to the present day, events calendar several times a day. On 102.2/102.8 FM.

Radio

- **www.onestives.co.uk:** Fantastic website by Steve McIntosh with lots of inside information, a constantly updated events calendar and helpful links, including for visitors thinking of moving to St Ives.

Websites

- **www.tripadvisor.com:** Independent assessment of hotels by visitors. Currently 450 reviews of 70 different places to stay in St Ives. Very helpful, as everything is laid bare.
- **www.stives–cornwall.co.uk:** Official website for St Ives in collaboration with the *St Ives Hotel & Guest House Association.* Accommodation divided into price categories and indicated on the town map.

- **www.visit-stives.co.uk:** Constantly updated information on beds available in the various types of accommodation.

St Ives alternative tourist guide

www.snottontv.co.uk
but it is on DVD
Contact for details: snottontv@gmail.co.uk

Beach

Deep blue and glistening gold are usually the first things visitors to St Ives notice. This is hardly surprising, as the town is surrounded by sea and sand. Together with nearby Carbis Bay, St Ives has **five greatly differing beaches** – it is as if nature has deliberately provided for different tastes. The individual beaches are also so close to each other that you can easily beach hop. Please note that dogs are banned from all beaches from Easter to 1st October.

PORTHMINSTER BEACH

Porthminster Beach is protected by St Ives Bay, thus **the sea here is usually calm**. This makes swimming safe for children, and it's why the beach is so popular amongst families.

For families and children

Best spot for sunrises, as the beach faces east and the sun thus seems to appear from the sea in a picturesque way.

There are a number of kiosks selling ice cream and snacks and hiring out deckchairs and windbreaks. Also a sort of putting green, a grassy area, a promenade and benches for everyone wanting a sea view without sand between their toes. The sun-drenched beach-side *Porthminster Café* (see 'Cafés' section) is highly recommended.

PORTHMEOR BEACH

For surfers

Facing the Atlantic and thus the **wildest of all the beaches**, with high waves and a lot of surfers. Embedded as it is between the Island to the east, Man's Head point to the west and Tate St Ives behind it, Porthmeor Beach has been the inspiration for countless paintings.

The beach is **totally surf oriented**, with a surf school, board hire and lifeguards. Despite this you don't get the mayhem of Newquay; everything is somehow more relaxed and more ‚serious' – in the positive sense.

There are two kiosks, a shop selling beach articles and deckchair hire. And of course there's the *Porthmeor Beach Café*, from the terrace of which you can experience **one of the best sunsets in St Ives.** Or just plant yourself on the beach in the evening with a rug, a picnic and a bottle of wine.

Beach aficionado
For **Gina Thomas** there's nothing to beat Porthmeor Beach.

'The beach is better than any pub,' she says, *'especially in the evening. In the summer we light a camp fire here nearly every night. Tourists are always coming and joining in.'* And that's precisely what Gina likes. *'Within a week you can always make new friends.'*
When Gina was eleven she and her parents moved to St Ives, and three years later they moved away again, to Wales. Two years ago she came back and stayed. *'It was always an inner compulsion – I just had to come back.'*

PORTHGWIDDEN BEACH

For romantics

A good way to start the day. Nobody bathing in the clear and usually cold water of Porthgwidden and warmed by the rays of the early-morning sun can deny that this spot is **like paradise**. Betwixt the rocks and the Island everything seems right with the world. After a swim you can enjoy a generous breakfast in the *Porthgwidden Café* (see section 'Restaurants'), from where you can watch the **smallest of the St Ives bays** slowly fill up with people. A kiosk provides visiting romantics with coffee and snacks.

HARBOUR BEACH

For people watchers

See and be seen: This is where you go if you just want to sun yourself for a while or compete for a Cornish pasty with the greedy gulls. You can either sit in the sand (only possible at low tide) or relax on a bench or deckchair and watch the **brightly coloured fishing boats** and the busy harbour life. At very low tides you can even walk through the sand to Porthminster Beach.

The harbour beach is also particularly **protected from the wind**; the calmest spot is below the pier, with the pier behind you as a wind protector.

CARBIS BAY

For relaxation seekers

Carbis Bay is about 1.5 miles from St Ives, and is easily reachable in half an hour on the coast path. It is **calmer** here than in busy St Ives. The sand of this long sandy beach seems **particularly fine and golden**, and the sea is calm and thus ideal for wind surfers, water skiers and families with children. In the summer lifeguards are in attendance, and there is a beach shop.

SURFING

You can hardly imagine St Ives without somebody walking around with a board under his arm. Tate St Ives doesn't have cycle racks – it instead has holders where you can leave surfboards.

St Ives Surf School

Everybody's gone surfin', surfin'... St Ives. Situated on Porthmeor Beach, this is THE place for surfers and anyone wanting to try and ride the waves. Dean and the others teach beginners and advanced surfers, in groups or individually. All surfing teachers are RLSS lifeguards with qualifications from the *British Surfing Association*.

What?

From £25 for 2 hrs including equipment. Hire of surfboards/body boards/wetsuits £4 for 2 hrs, £6 for 4 hrs and £7 for a whole day.

How much?

Daily from June to October. In July/August it's best to book 2–3 days in advance.

When?

On Porthmeor Beach, Tel. 0779-2261278.

Where?

Porthmeor Beach

waiting for the perfect wave

Living to surf
Dean Mackay is a surfing teacher at *St Ives Surf School* who was born in St Ives and has grown up with the waves.

How long have you been surfing? I started when I was 13.

What's the best thing about Porthmeor Beach? It's beautiful, clean and only five minutes from the town centre. And it's less over-run than Newquay.

Is Porthmeor best for beginners or advanced surfers? Both. Just after high tide is the best time for beginners and low tide is best for advanced surfers.

Where can you go to wind-surf? Marazion, near Penzance.

Surf shops　Every other shop in Fore Street is a surf shop. They're all pretty much of a muchness – the best thing is to go and look at them yourself. It's more practical and no more expensive to hire equipment when you get to Porthmeor Beach.

Surfing weather
- **Seasalt:** Clothes shop at 4 Fore Street (near Market Place) that displays daily updated information outside on a big light-blue board, namely air and water temperatures, wind speed and direction, wave height and high- and low tide times.
- **www.a1surf.com/surfcheck-porthmeor.html:** Current information on wind and weather on Porthmeor Beach. With tide table and helpful comments such as ‚Don't bother!'.
- **Surfcall:** Surfing conditions in the southwest on Tel. 09068-360360.

Activities

WALKING

You could hardly imagine a better starting point for walks than St Ives. It is right on the South West Coast Path, and in a few minutes you can be in the middle of unspoilt nature with hair-raising cliff drops, crashing waves, screeching gulls, lonely coves and expansive dune landscapes.

One of the most beautiful sections of coast in Cornwall
To Zennor
Distance: approx. 7 miles.
NB: Walk one way, then return by bus or taxi (in 10 min.). Not recommended if it has been raining – the path may then be pretty boggy.

Tate St Ives is the starting point. Walk westwards for a few minutes along the Porthmeor Beach promenade, until the coast path starts on your right – you can't miss it.

After a short while you'll come to the headland **Clodgy Point**, from where you can look back on St Ives one last time and take in the wonderful view of the town, Porthmeor Beach and the Island.

From now on the path goes constantly up and down through the wilderness, from headland to headland, past **Hor Point** and **Pen Enys Point** (National Trust path markings). The coast path is well signposted, so you'll have no problems finding your way – just keep the sea on your right!

A few minutes after a plank path comes the Trevalgan Farm Trail, which leads inland. But keep to the right and you'll arrive at a superb **picnic area** with wooden tables, high above the sea and looking down onto a tiny cove.

You then have to scramble over rocks – concentration required – until the next headland, **Carn Naun Point**, which is the **halfway point to Zennor**.

The path now goes down almost to sea level, across a stream, after which it's a steep uphill scramble. Not far from this there's a fork going inland through Treveal valley, which you should ignore.

Just off the coast you can now see the rocky reef of the Carracks, also known as **Seal Island. Seals** can often be seen here; they're visible with the naked eye, but binoculars are helpful.

The next headland is not Zennor Head but **Mussel Point**. Getting round it involves a lot of climbing up and down, before you at last get

your first proper view of **Zennor Head.** There's then quite a walk up- and downhill until the path finally turns off to the left and leads into a narrow street. On the finishing straight we go past the sweet little vil- lage church dating from the 15th century (with its famous *Mermaid of Zennor* carving), then at last you can stretch your weary limbs and en- joy a cool pint in the **Tinners Arms.**

Zennor is a most beautiful place: *a tiny granite village nes- tling under high shaggy moor-hills and a big sweep of lovely sea beyond,* **lovelier even than the Mediterranean** ... *It is the best place I have been in, I think.'*
D.H. Lawrence (1916)

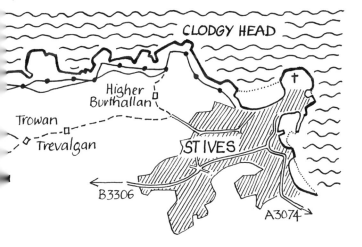

Tinners Arms

What? Time seems to have stopped in Zennor's only pub. It was built in 1271 of solid stone, and in the winter there are two open fires. There's no loud music here, no TV sport and not even a mobile signal. Instead there's tasty food and a terrace with a view of the Atlantic. Watch the sun set beyond the horizon!

How much? Main meals £6 to £15.

When? In the summer Mon–Sat 11am–11pm, Sun 12–10.30pm. In the winter closed between 3pm and 6.30pm. Lunch 12–2.30pm, evening meals 6.30–9pm.

Where? Right in the middle of the village – you can't miss it. Tel. 01736 796927, www.tinnersarms.com.

old tin mine

Birds and dunes
To Godrevy Point
Distance: approx. 10 miles.
NB: Walk there and return by taxi. Alternatively, to shorten the walk start in Hayle, i.e. drive (see below) or take the No. 14 bus to Hayle (15 min.) or the *St Ives Bay Holiday Camp* stop near the Towans (20 min.).

Walk past **Porthminster Beach** on the coast path, which here is still asphalted, until after half an hour you reach the long, fine sandy beach of **Carbis Bay**. **Trencrom Hill** is ¾ mile south of Carbis Bay, and is one of the best **vantage points** in West Cornwall, offering views over St Ives Bay to the north and Mounts Bay to the south.

Keep to the South West Coast Path, which now loops inland past **Lelant** to cross the **River Hayle**. On the road between Lelant und Hayle

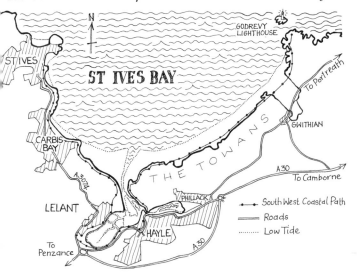

is the **Old Quay House Inn**, where you can take a break. It is also suitable as a starting point for a section of the walk (car park with information building).

Before the estuary pretty much silted up, Hayle was one of the most important harbours in Cornwall, above all for tin export. There is now an area of mud flats – the **Saltings** – at the river estuary, where **extreme tidal flows** can be observed. This conservation area is a **resting place for numerous migratory birds** from the Arctic (spring and autumn) and a summer breeding ground for shore birds.

After crossing the river the coast path goes back towards the sea and into the miles of beautiful **dune landscape** called the **Towans** – take your shoes off and walk barefoot through the sand! The next 3 miles will take you past various camp sites and finally the village of **Gwithian**, picturesquely embedded in the sand dunes.

The next headland is **Godrevy Point**, the site of the famous/infamous white lighthouse which was Virginia Woolf's inspiration for her novel *To the Lighthouse*. It was built in 1859 to prevent the frequent shipwrecks caused by the reefs and shallows. **Godrevy Lighthouse** is now powered by solar energy, and its surroundings are home to cormorants, oystercatchers and grey seals. From the car park a short path (4-5 minutes) cuts across the headland to a deep and inaccessible cove where you **can usually see seals – sometimes up to 100** of them – hauling out on the beach.

Godrevy Point can also be reached by car. Turn off the B3301 ¾ mile north of Gwithian, immediately after crossing a small bridge, and drive down the narrow road for about 1¼ miles until you reach the National Trust car park.

Further walks

Tinner's Way

The cross-country section from St Ives to Zennor is part of the so-called Tinner's Way, which was used for transportation of tin and copper. You can start from the *Garrack Hotel* in St Ives and either walk from farm to farm to Zennor or take one of the various paths branching off towards the coast, creating a circular route (outward on the Tinner's Way and back on the coast path).

Information: a good description of the path is to be found at www.onestives.co.uk (under *walks*).

St Michael's Way

From St Ives to Marazion and St Michael's Mount on the former pilgrims' route (see chapter 'Excursions'). It's 12½ miles from the north to the south coast of Cornwall.

Information: the brochure *St Michael's Way* (£2), complete with maps and a detailed description of the path, is available from the Tourist Information Centre.

Literature for walkers

- **The South West Coast Path Guide:** Brought out by the *South West Coast Path Association* and updated annually, including detailed descriptions of paths, tide tables and timetables, £8.50. Tel. 01752-896237, www.swcp.org.uk.
- **Margaret Sharp:** *20 short walks around St Ives:* simply described walks around St Ives und Zennor, £2.99. In every book shop in St Ives or at www.stivesnews.co.uk (under *book shop*).

GUIDED WALKS
Columbus Walks

What? Walks and plenty of information on fishermen, artists, cats and canons. Whether you want an interesting two-hour guided tour of the town or a cliff walk to Seal Island – no group is too small for this 'explorer'.

How much? £3-7.50 per walk, accompanied children free of charge.

Where? Tel. 07980-149243.

RIDING
Old Mill Stables

What? Riding stables since 1962. Beginners and advanced riders of all ages can ride through moors, woods and fields. Special half-hour courses for children (5–6 years). Maximum weight 80 kg, riding hats for hire free of charge. Ring in advance.

How much? £15 for about an hour in groups, £25/hr individual tuition.

Where? Lelant Downs, near Hayle, opposite *St Ives Holiday Village*. Tel. 01736-753045.

Penhalwyn Trekking Centre

What? Rides through the moors, past historic sites, individually or in groups. Half-day or whole-day rides also possible, all levels and all ages. Book in advance.

How much? £15/hr in groups, £30/hr individual tuition.

Where? In Halsetown, 1½ miles from St Ives on the B3311 towards Penzance. Tel. 01736-796461.

DIVING
Dive St Ives

Cornwall's underwater world may not compete with the reefs of the Caribbean, but the environs of St Ives are an **oasis for wreck divers**. The most famous shipwreck is the *St Chamond*, which sunk 1½ miles off St Ives in 1918 and is loaded with six surprisingly well preserved steam locomotives. Wreck diving is just one of the specialities offered by the friendly Dive St Ives team. They also offer boat diving, deep-sea diving and night diving, plus the standard *Open Water Diver* training for beginners as well as *Divemaster* and *Assistant Instructor* courses. Also snorkelling trips to Godrevy Lighthouse or Seal Island. Shop and repairs.

What?

Open Water Diver from £299, *Divemaster* £349, *Assistant Instructor* £229 (the latter without course pack and equipment). Hire of complete equipment £40 (also individual parts), snorkelling £20.

How much?

Summer daily 9am–9pm, winter 11am–5pm.

When?

25 Wharf Road, Tel. 01736-799229, www.divestives.com.

Where?

SAILING TRIPS
St Ives Bay Sailing

They offer everything from short cruises across the bay to three day trips to the Isles of Scilly. **Seals, dolphins and even sharks** can often be seen along what is one of the most precipitous sections of coast in West Cornwall. Complete safety equipment, tea/coffee/biscuits and occasionally Cornish pasties are available on board, or, depending on the time of day, a cream tea.

What?

How much?	£30 for 2 hrs, £45 for 4 hrs, £70 for a whole day. Prices per person based on at least three participants.
Where?	2 Molteno Place, Tel. 07971-775228, www.stivesbay sailing.co.uk.

BOAT TRIPS

Tickets for ½- to 1-hr trips to Seal Island to see the seals or for mackerel fishing are available by the harbour, where you'll find people standing around peddling these excursions. You can also hire a motorboat (£15 for ½ hr, £20/hr – maximum five people).

Shopping

PRESENTS
Craftys Country Store
Country house style needn't be old-fashioned: materials, quilts, writing paper, address books – sometimes
rustic, sometimes with a lighter touch and sort of
French inspired. A little corner with artists' materials.
In the summer 9.30am–9.30pm, otherwise 9.30am–
5.30pm.
54 Fore Street, www.craftyscountrystore.com.

What?

When?

Where?

The Glass Tree
Small corner shop jam-packed with beautiful things.
Creamy-white decorative items, cups, bowls, book
marks and a huge selection of *Pilgrim* jewellery. Experiment: Keep dead quiet and just listen – I'll bet
you that the hearts of any women in the room will be
beating at double speed.
Mon–Sat 10.30am–5pm, Sun closed. In the winter
the opening times may vary.
The Digey, corner of Love Lane. www.theglasstree.
co.uk.

What?

When?

Where?

Top 5 St Ives souvenirs

- Sue Lewington's book *A day in St Ives*, with its achingly beautiful illustrations.
- Scone mixture from *Pengenna Pasties* (High Street).
- Striped egg cups from the *fish pye pottery* (Back Road East). Make sure you don't get a bantam-size one!
- DVD of the comedy troupe *Kulture Brake* (available at the Arts Club/Westcott's Quay or at bmoodypoet@aol.com).
- A print (etching/silkscreen/collographs) from the *Printmakers' Gallery* (Tregenna Hill).

PHOTOS
St Ives Photographics: Automatic digital photos here 39p each (cf. 49p at *Boots*, where USB sticks cannot be read), Wharf Road.

St Ives Camera Company: Fore Street, next to the *Seafood Café*.

CLOTHES
West Coast
You can find things that are IN and wearable here, **What?** including brands such as *Emily the Strange* and *Ichi*. For men and women, including shoes and various accessories.

July–Sept daily 9.30am–9.30pm, otherwise Mon–Sat **When?** 10am–5pm, Sun 11am–4pm.

18 Fore Street. **Where?**

Clotworthy's
Unprepossessing externally, but inside there's a good **What?** range of clothes by *Bench, French Connection* and the Cornish surf brand *Hager-Vor*.

Daily 10am–5.30pm, in the summer until 10pm. **When?**

Wharf Road. **Where?**

CHILDREN
Fabulous Kids

What? Clothes, shoes and much more that you don't need but really want. Everything is strangely attractive – even to non-mothers. Dummies with skull print, dinosaur finger puppets, socks packed as flowers. Not cheap, but nice.

When? In the summer daily from 10am–9.30pm, otherwise 10am–5pm.

Where? 40 Fore Street, www.fabulouskids.co.uk.

More shopping
- Book shops in the chapter 'Literature'.
- Craft work in the chapter 'Art'.
- Food shopping/delis in the chapter 'Food'.

Going out

If you're expecting to experience a wild party life in St Ives you'll be disappointed. Thankfully there's no rowdy night-time atmosphere like you get in the surfing stronghold Newquay (35 miles away). St Ives is more tranquil – traditional pubs dominate the night life, jazz and blues are heard more than dance rhythms, and quality ales are preferred to cocktails and sickly alcopops.

The pub scene in St Ives is pretty impressive. The pubs are relaxed meeting places for locals and tourists, offer a wide range of ales, serve surprisingly good food, are venues for convivial gatherings and provide plenty of live music (see the chapter 'Music').

But club sounds and trendy bars are gradually coming to St Ives, doubtless as a consequence of the opening of the Backpacker hostel – THE place for surfers to stay.

The bar/club *Isobar* opened in 1997, and it remains St Ives' only nightclub. 2003 saw the advent of the *Hub*, a bar with lounge, and two years later came the *Blue Bar*. And that's basically it as far as cocktails and dancing are concerned.

PUBS
Quaint old haunt
Sloop Inn
One of the oldest pubs in the whole of Cornwall (dating from about 1312). The building, stooping under the force of the wind, with low ceilings and full of nooks and crannies, provides a charmingly cosy at-

What?

mosphere. Big range of good food – especially fresh fish. Free Internet access using your own laptop (Wi-Fi hot spot), plus changing exhibitions by local artists.

Why? Because you can wallow in the romance of this quaint old harbour haunt, which has provided the setting for various films. The patio area outside is an ideal spot for people watching.

Who? Sooner or later everyone ends up in the Sloop. You'll meet a lot of locals and artists here.

How much? The prices of up to £2.85 a pint reflect the location. Food for between £4 (sandwich) und £10 (steak).

When? Breakfast 9–11am, bar meals 12–3pm and 5–9.30pm. Alcohol from 10am to midnight.

Where? Harbour front, The Wharf, Tel. 01736-796584 (also for the pub's Bed & Breakfast), www.sloop-inn.co.uk.

Exciting range of ales
Castle Inn

The only pub with such a wide and regularly chang-   **What?**
ing range of real ales. In the summer there are always
five or six, and in winter three or four. The Castle
also puts on an Easter Beer Festival, at which there
are even more ales to try out (50 different ones over
the course of a week or so). Tip: They always have at
least one of the excellent ales by *Skinners* (brewery in
Truro/Cornwall).

Something to think about: Why should there only be   **Why?**
wine tastings?

Beer connoisseurs and lovers of the typically dark and   **Who?**
cosy pub atmosphere.

A pint costs between £2.50 and £2.70.   **How much?**

11am to midnight, Fridays and Saturdays until 1am.   **When?**
Food available from Easter to the end of September.

16 Fore Street.   **Where?**

BAR
Beautiful people on beautiful balcony
Hub

Trendy bar with restaurant. Downstairs a big cock-   **What?**
tail bar, and upstairs a cosy lounge with a master-
ly mix of old and new furniture. DJs above all play
funky house (house music without any extreme bass
lines or endless loops, often with vocals), on Sundays
more chilled-out soul. Regular live music à la Jack
Johnson.

Because the Hub has one of the best balconies, with a   **Why?**
transparent balustrade for an unrestricted view of the
harbour. Also a nice place for a coffee.

Who?	Very varied, depending on time of day and season. In the daytime absolutely anyone, evenings/nights lots of beautiful people in skimpy clothing. Out of season more relaxed.
How much?	£2.80–£3.30 a pint.
When?	Open from 10am, 10–11.30am breakfast, hot food in the summer until 5pm. Weekends open until midnight.
Where?	4 Wharf Road.

CLUB
Watch out for bouncers
Isobar

What?	St Ives' only nightclub. Divided into two levels: downstairs bar, burgers and screens for sports broadcasts, upstairs dance floor and laser show. Chiefly charts und funky house, Fridays live music (watch the postings).
Why?	Because there's no alternative if you want to dance.
Who?	Typical party people, young and hip. Says Mohan Scott (27, St Ives): 'The people there are too young for me.' Clothes and drugs check at the door – no admission if you're wearing a hat.
How much?	£2.50–£2.90 a pint. Admission £3 to £6, free before 10pm. Drink promotions, e.g. drinks for £1 on Wednesdays.
When?	Open every day in the summer, in the winter Thur/Fri/Sat from 7pm. Food served until 2am.
Where?	Street-an-Pol, www.theisobar.co.uk.

Excursions

Shakespeare by starlight
Minack Theatre

Open-air theatre high above the sea, nestled in the steep granite cliffs. For nearly fifty years Rowena Cade and a single assistant cut the stage and seating into the cliffs on her land with their own hands. Shakespeare's *The Tempest* was the first performance here in 1932, and the theatre now stages 18 plays a season. The thundering of the waves, the sunset and the starry sky become part and parcel of the performance – a unique experience.

What?

Evenings Mon–Fri and matinees Wed & Fri June to Sept. Open to visitors all year round.

When?

The Minack Theatre

How much?	Tickets £7.50, under-16s £4. Day visitors £3, under-16s £1.20, free of charge for the under-12s.
Where?	Porthcurno – follow the signs. By car via Penzance approx. 30 min. It's nicer to take the coast road via St Just (50 min.). By bus (No. 1 or No. 345) from Penzance to Porthcurno (35-60 min.), and from there about ¼ mile walk up the steep hill – plan return bus journey in advance. Tel. 01736-810181, www.minack.com.

Minack survival kit

- Cushion (otherwise unbearable sitting on the cold, hard stones). Or: for £1 you can hire an excellent cushion/backrest at Minack.
- Rug (even in the summer it can get pretty chilly in the evening)
- Thick pullover, jacket, and perhaps scarf and gloves*
- Umbrella (capes available at the theatre)
- Sunscreen for matinees
- Hot drink in a thermos
- Bottle of wine, corkscrew and glasses
- Picnic

*the author admittedly feels the cold

Living like lords
St Michael's Mount

What? About 400 m off the Cornish coast the English twin of France's Norman monastery Mont Saint Michel rises proudly from its granite base. In 1050 the Benedictine monks were bequeathed this rocky islet, where they erected the counterpart of their abbey in France. It has since become a pilgrimage station on the Way of St James to Santiago de Compostela. It later became a fort, and latterly a private dwelling. Beautiful rock garden.

Castle: April–Oct, Mon–Fri and Sun; Garden: May/June Mon–Fri, July–Oct Thur and Fri only. Always 10.30am–5.30pm (last entry 4.45pm). **When?**

Castle: £6.40, children £3.20. Garden: £3, children £1. Family and group tickets. Boat crossing at high tide £1.20. **How much?**

From Penzance 3 miles eastwards on the A30 to the roundabout, then right exit onto the A394, signposted Marazion. Or by No. 300 bus from St Ives to Marazion. Then walk over the causeway (15 min.) at low tide, or take the boat at high tide. Tel. 01736-710507, www.stmichaelsmount.co.uk. **Where?**

Underground and under the sea
Geevor Tin Mine

UK's biggest preserved tin mine, worked until 1990. Museum and interesting tour of the workings, some of which extend deep below the sea. **What?**

Daily except Sat Easter–Oct: from 9am with hourly tours of the workings 10am–4pm. In the winter entry until 3pm, tours at 11am, 1pm and 3pm. **When?**

£7.50, OAPs £7, children and students £4.30. **How much?**

Pendeen, 7 miles west of Penzance. From St Ives on the B3306 coast road, past Zennor and Morvah to Pendeen. In the summer the No. 300 bus (often open-top) plies the same route – in the winter first to Penzance, then change to the No. 17. Let the driver know in advance that you want to get off at Geevor Tin Mine. Tel. 01736-788662, www.geevor.com. **Where?**

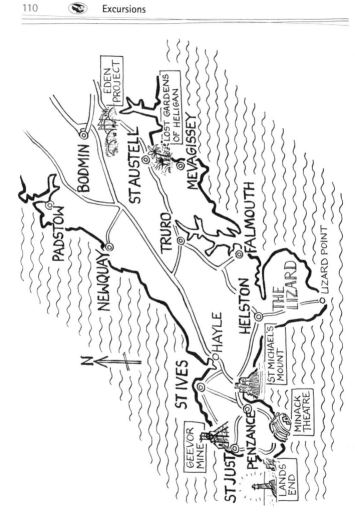

**From St Ives to St Just –
'UK's best scenic drive'**

If you're going to Geevor Tin Mine or the Minack Theatre you're strongly urged to take the coast road via Zennor, which offers breathtaking views of the wild cliff landscape. St Ives' very own **poet, comedian and musician Rod Bullimore** even goes as far as to describe the route as the most scenic drive in Britain.

Rod came down from Lincolnshire in 1994 and stayed put: *'I came to St Ives as a child, and ever since then I'd had this diffuse idea in my head that I wanted to return.'*

You can always see and hear this all-round talent somewhere in town (especially in the Arts Club, with its comedy troupe *Kulture Brake*, in the *Salthouse Gallery* or in the various pubs).

A machete instead of a kiss – the Sleeping Beauty lives!
Lost Gardens of Heligan

Enchanted garden of the Tremayne family, who re-   What?
sided here for 400 years. 22 gardeners used to keep the 32 hectares in shape, but after WW1 the garden became increasingly overgrown. Rescue came in 1990 in the form of the Dutch **rock musician Tim Smit**, botanist und friend of the Heligan heir John Willis. Beneath the stinging nettles and ivy Smit found a botanic treasure trove and **brought the 'lost gardens' back to life**. This reconstruction of the original gardens now offers an enchanted primeval forest com-

plete with bamboos and palms, an Italian garden with giant sized courgettes and a lost valley.

When? March–Oct daily 10am–6pm (entry until 4.30pm), Nov–Feb daily 10am–5pm (entry until 3.30pm).

How much? £7.50, OAPs £7, children (5–16) £4, under-5s free of charge. Family and group tickets available.

Where? Near St Austell, from where you should take the B3273 towards Mevagissey, then follow the signs to Heligan. By public transport: to St Austell either by *National Express* coach (about 80 min.) or train (about 70 min.). From St Austell about 35 min. by *First* bus No. 25 or *Western Greyhound* bus No. 526. Tel. 01726-845100, www.heligan.com.

Rainy day programme
Eden Project

What? The **biggest greenhouses in the world** proudly project from the Cornish soil like some kind of futuristic giant honeycomb. The Eden millennium project was realised for £76m in 2001, to a design by the star architect Nicholas Grimshaw. Eden has over a million plants, and the eight enormous greenhouses represent the earth's various climate zones. Eleven double-decker buses stacked on top of each other or the entire Tower of London would fit into the biggest of the greenhouses. Every year 1.25 million visitors experience the link between nature and technology here (though the vast amounts of electricity consumed do not come from alternative sources).

When? April–Oct 9am–6pm (entry until 4.30pm), Nov–March 10am–4.30pm (entry until 3pm).

How much? £13.80, OAPs £10, students £7, children (5–18) £5, under-5s free of charge. Reductions for groups of ten or more to be booked in advance.

Four miles from St Austell. Special buses from St
Austell station. By car A30 to Innis Downs roundabout, then follow the signs. Tel. 01726-811911, www.
edenproject.com.

Where?

Don't bother!
Land's End
It could be so lovely breathing in the cool air of the
westernmost point of the English mainland. But instead of a wild and romantic experience you'll find
a dreadful amusement park: The Land's End Experience. What's available outside for free is unconvinc-
ingly imitated using **artificial background sounds
and trivial laser effects**. There are busloads of tourists tripping up over each other, crowding around the
souvenirs and queuing to have their photo taken. It's

What?

a waste of time! But if you do want to visit Land's End there's nothing to stop you approaching it free of charge along the cliff path. A good half hour from Sennen Cove/Whitesand Bay. Or try Cape Cornwall instead!

Excursions made easy
Oates Travel

What? All manner of excursions from St Ives, e.g. Lizard peninsula, *Lost Gardens of Heligan*, *Eden Project*, Polperro and King Arthur's castle ruins in Tintagel. Highly recommended, as you avoid the many annoying changes of public transport – especially for the trip to the *Minack Theatre*, from where it's hard to get any other transport late in the evening. Tickets arranged as part of package.

When? Times always displayed in the window.

How much? Minack £16, Heligan £17, Eden £21 – entrance fees included.

Where? 1 High Street, Tel. 01736-795343.

A to Z of Tips for Visitors

Barclays, Lloyds TSB, HSBC and *Halifax* in High Street and **Banks**
NatWest in Gabriel Street.

Buses and coaches depart from The Malakoff/Fernlea Ter- **Buses/**
race. Bus timetables available from the TIC (Tourist Infor- **Coaches**
mation Centre), *Ace Cars* (taxi company right next to the
bus station), on Tel. 01872-322003 or at www.cornwall.
gov.uk/buses. Travel information on Tel. 0870-6082608.

- *St Ives Car Hire*, Tel. 0845-0579373, www.stivescarhire. **Car Hire**
  co.uk.
- *St Ives Motor Company*, on the road to Carbis Bay, Tel.
  01736-796695, www.stivesmotor.co.uk.

There are several public car parks: The Island, Porth- **Car Parks**
gwidden, Porthmeor, Barnoon (on the hill over Porthmeor
Beach), the station (behind Porthminster Beach), behind
the *Sloop Inn*, Smeaton's Pier, Park Avenue and Upper
Trenwith. There are regular buses from Royal Square (opposite the cinema) serving the higher car parks.

The Tourist Information Centre stocks the brochure *A* **Disabilities**
Guide for the Less Abled Visitor. All the beaches have
wheelchair ramps, Tate St Ives has a lift and many hotels and restaurants are equipped for people with disabilities.

- **GPs:** *Stennack Surgery*, The Stennack, Tel. 01736- **Doctors/**
  793333 or -796413.   **Dentists/**
- **Dentists:** *Poznansky & Franklyn*, Tregenna Hill, Tel.   **Vets**

01736-796260; *Burgess*, 6-7 Boskerris Terrace/Carbis Bay, Tel. 01736-793090.

- **Vet:** *St Ives Veterinary Surgery*, Trenwith Lane, Tel. 01736-798333.

Emergency Services   999 – police, fire, ambulance and coastwatch.

Gay Scene   St Ives does not exactly offer much for homosexuals. Some B&Bs are expressly gay-friendly, e.g. the *White Wave Guest House* (see chapter 'Accommodation'). Otherwise see www.gaycornwall.com.

Hospital   Edward Hain Hospital, Albany Terrace, Tel. 01736-576100.

Internet   There is no dedicated Internet café in St Ives, but there are the following possibilities:

- Library: First ½ hour free, then £2/hr for members and £3 for non-members. Anyone can join free of charge. Tue 9.30am–9.30pm, Wed Fri 9.30am-8pm (winter until 6pm), Sat 9.30am-12.30pm, Sun and Mon closed. Gabriel Street.
- *Dive St Ives*: First 20 min. £1, then 5p/min. (= £3/hr). Summer daily 9am-9pm, winter 11am-5pm. 25 Wharf Road.

Launderette   St Ives Launderette, 9 Alma Terrace/The Stennack, Tel. 01736-796071.

Leisure Centre   Leisure Centre with swimming pool and fitness studio (55 items of equipment) by Higher Trenwith car park. Regular buses from/to Royal Square. Mon–Fri 6.30am–10pm,

Sat–Sun 7am–5.30pm. The swimming pool is used by school classes 9am–12pm and 1.30–3.30pm. Tel. 01736-797006.

- *The Garage*, Parc-an-Creet/Higher Stennack, on the road to Zennor.
- *St Ives Motor Company*, on the road to Carbis Bay.

Petrol Stations

- *Boots*, 3 High Street, Tel. 01736-795072.
- *Leddra Chemists*, Fore Street, Tel. 01736-795432.
- *Stennack Pharmacy*, The Stennack, Tel. 01736-795047.

Pharmacies

Tregenna Hill, Market Place, next to the cinema (Royal Square), *Sloop Inn* car park, St Ives Museum, Tate St Ives, Porthmeor Hill.

Phone Boxes

Dove Street, behind the cinema, Tel. 08705-777444.

Police

Main post office: 11 Tregenna Hill. Branch post offices: Fore Street/corner of The Wharf; 1 Fern Glen/The Stennack; St Ives Road/Carbis Bay.

Post Offices

Available at the Tourist Information Centre for 20p.

Street-Maps

- *Ace Cars*, Tel. 01736-797779.
- *D. J. Cars*, Tel. 01736-796633.
- *Goodways Cars*, Tel. 01736-794437.
Taxi rank beside the cinema

Taxis

Street-an-Pol, Tel. 01736-796297.

TIC (Tourist Information Centre)

Toilets   Public toilets: Porthminster Beach, Porthmeor car park, Porthgwidden, behind the *Sloop Inn*, behind the lifeboat station, Smeaton's Pier.

Trains   The station is behind Porthminster Beach. Big car park. Train information either at the station or on Tel. 08457-484950. www.nationalrail.co.uk.

Weddings   St Ives seems extremely marriage oriented, and offers a number of venues. Information at www.stives-cornwall. co.uk/weddings.html and Penzance Register Office, Tel. 01736-330093.

When to Come   There's not really a 'best time' to visit St Ives, as it depends what is important to the individual.
   The climate is influenced by the Gulf Stream, which gives rise to a long summer and a mild winter. The Atlantic creates moderate heat and regular rainfall equally distributed throughout the year – hence the deep green of the landscape. In the summer months the rainfall is usually only brief, and the weather can change by the minute, but in the winter it can rain for days (January comes top of the league with 19 days of rain). In April/May everything is in bloom, so this is the best time for garden-lovers to come.
   St Ives remains relatively quiet until the end of June, in July/August British and continental tourists storm the town. September is calmer again, excepting during the September Festival in the middle two weeks, when there are a lot of visitors. September enjoys the same average temperatures as June (approx. 17 °C), the difference being that the sea warms up during the summer – though 'warm up' is to be taken with a pinch of salt.

INDEX

We need you!

Things are always in flux in St Ives and the vicinity – as indeed everywhere – and we would be grateful for any information. Have prices (dramatically) increased, does a restaurant no longer exist, or is a once good hotel suddenly bad? Any feedback, comments, suggestions and criticisms will be most welcome.

We would also like to know about your favourite places, walks, trips, B & Bs, shops etc.

Many thanks!

goldfinch books
Muehlendamm 53
22087 Hamburg
Germany   talk2us@goldfinchbooks.de

Name and address: